Noooo!
I'm Not a
Cartoon Character

Noooo!
I'm Not a
Cartoon Character

LIZ LALLY

iUniverse LLC
Bloomington

NOOOO! I'M NOT A CARTOON CHARACTER

iUniverse books may be ordered through booksellers or by contacting:

iUniverse LLC
1663 Liberty Drive
Bloomington, IN 47403
www.iuniverse.com
1-800-Authors (1-800-288-4677)

ISBN: 978-1-4917-0251-2 (sc)
ISBN: 978-1-4917-0252-9 (ebk)

Library of Congress Control Number: 2013914335

Printed in the United States of America

iUniverse rev. date: 08/08/2013

To my family and friends who encouraged me to write this book and especially my husband, Thomas, who was the inspiration of my stories.

Contents

Introduction

Some friends we knew forever were gathered on our deck for a picnic. Well into the evening someone remarked, "Liz, you and Tom are two of a kind and definitely *Cartoon Characters*." I shouted, "No, I am not like Tom and certainly not a *Cartoon Character!*" Everyone replied in unison, "Yes, you are!"

Two years ago, I wrote a whole book about the things that provoked me about Tom. It was titled *Help! I Married a Cartoon Character*. How could I possibly be compared to someone who was the opposite of me in so many ways? I couldn't imagine why they thought I was a personality like Tom. He was the character with the oddball logic and cartoonish behavior, not me.

At first, I was in complete denial that I may be a cartoon character. However, after much soul searching, I remembered while I was writing the book, Tom would occasionally ask, "What about the time you did this or that?" I responded, "The book is about you, *not me*." I continued reminiscing about my life and realized some things about myself that may be considered a little cartoony. Then I realized these same friends that were accusing me of being a cartoon character were with me and sometimes the cause of many of my encounters. Of course, Tom continued his comical behavior and my relatives were doing things that one might consider comic as well. Everywhere I went I observed people walking into doors, getting into the wrong cars, and snow falling off roofs onto their heads.

I revealed the humorous, true, and cartoony adventures of myself, family, relatives, friends, and the people around me. These stories are the true test of our for-better-or-worse vows. I am sure everyone can relate to these adventures. I have discovered there is a little cartoon character in all of us.

1

The Rude Awakening

One summer evening, some of our friends were gathered on our deck for a friendly get-together and even though it had been two years since I wrote the book about my husband, Tom, titled *"Help I Married a Cartoon Character,"* they were still talking about Tom's adventures. They were discussing the "Lally Logic" of their hero when one of the fellows bellowed, "Liz, you and Tom are two of a kind and definitely are *Cartoon Characters."* I frantically responded, "Nooo! Don't say that! That can't be true! I am in no way like Tom." Everyone laughed and nodded in agreement. Just the thought of being a cartoon character horrified me!

After everyone had gone home, their comments still haunted me. I began thinking about what could have possibly brought them to that conclusion. I could understand why they thought Tom was a cartoon character because it was quite obvious that he was a little looney and definitely quite cartoony. Tom had already accepted the fact that he was one, but I just couldn't understand why they looked at me in that way. How could I possibly be a character that annoyed me so much? I asked Tom if he thought I was a cartoon character and he alleged with a blunt logic, "Certainty! How could you be any other character?" I thought, "What do my friends clearly see that is quite foggy to me?"

Try as I might, I just couldn't get the possibility out of my mind that over the years I could have been slowly turning into a cartoon character. Or was I always one? I remembered how Tom kept reminding me of the things I had done when I was writing the book about him. I would always declare, "This book is about you, *not me!*" Now our friends got me to thinking for the first time that just maybe I had slowly transformed into a cartoon character just like Tom. Most of our friends knew me since grade school, so I wondered if they noticed me morphing into this personality as early as that. I mused over my life in a futile attempt to discover if, how, or when I turned into a cartoon character. I decided to take a journey down memory lane and see if there was a cartoony path I took occasionally. As I was traveling back in time a vision flashed through my mind; I was two years old, a little knock-kneed and pigeon-toed. I wore gold, thick, bent, wire-rimmed safety glasses. Maybe I wasn't a cartoon character, but I sure looked like one. This vision led me to ponder over my life experiences that may be interpreted as a little cartoony; ones I never looked at in this way before. Stories immediately came to mind that were always told at family gatherings. Mom told the story of how I ran up and down the stairs of our apartment to tattle on my brother and cousins. I was only two years old and could hardly walk and talk. Then she revealed how I almost choked to death on crayons. After they retrieved the crayons from my throat, they asked, "Why on earth did you put crayons into your mouth?" I answered, "I was washing the crayons."

The next story happened when I was being a little nuisance at age three. My older cousin had enough of my antics, so he grabbed me and held my arms and legs so I couldn't move a muscle. I struggled to get free, but he held me so tight I couldn't escape his hold. After a while of me squirming to break free, he asked, "Now, what are you going to do?" There was only one way I could think of to break free, so without hesitation, I screamed, "I'm going to "shit" on you!" My response shocked him so much that he fell out of the chair bursting with laughter. Then I escaped his hold. He told this story at every family event.

Another favorite story was when Dad bought property and built a garage on the back of the lot, where we were to live until he built a house. I was only three when we moved into the garage. One day a neighbor, Merle, was standing in his yard and I went over to him and asked, "Do you know why we are living in a garage?" He answered, "No, why?" I replied, "Because my Dad is too dumb to build a house." He often told this story of how we first met.

Merle and his wife, Pansy, were in their forties and never had any children of their own, so they were thrilled when I moved into the neighborhood. They gave me plenty of attention and were intrigued by my antics. Pansy asked Mom if I could stay overnight whenever Merle worked the night shift. She didn't like to stay alone and enjoyed my company. I went every third week around 9:00 PM so I could watch television with them before he went to work. We didn't have television so this was a real treat, and she gave me a dollar when I stayed with her. She always said I could come earlier to watch television; however, Mom thought I would be too much of a nuisance (imagine that) and wouldn't let me go earlier. One day I got the bright idea of setting the clocks ahead an hour every evening after supper so I could go earlier and watch television. They were pleased to see me, and I enjoyed watching a couple more shows. I was clueless to how my action affected the rest of my family. Dad got up an hour earlier for work. At first they thought the clocks weren't working right. However, after a couple days of setting the clocks to the correct time and the next morning discovering all the clocks would be an hour ahead again, it didn't take them long to figure out I was the culprit. They weren't too happy. Mom asked, "Why did you do that? Your father got up and went to work an hour early every morning." I had to do some fast thinking, so I rationalized, "Well he went to bed an hour early so what's the problem? He got the same amount of sleep." However they didn't agree with my logic.

The next story concerns the same neighbors. Merle always invited my brother and me over to help him set up his train tracks and village at Christmas. He had quite a collection since he added to it every year. We helped arrange the track, houses, stores, and trees. I noticed he had everything imaginable except one thing, and the town wouldn't be complete without it. I thought, "This would be the perfect Christmas present for him."

I went shopping in downtown Sharon at the Murphy Store, and with my allowance I bought him a plastic miniature outhouse for his town. Being as inventive as I was at the time, I went one step further and put raisins in the outhouse so he would get the full effect. There was one more thing I needed to complete the outhouse; however, I couldn't find a catalog small enough to fit. I remembered my bad experience with the catalog in Grandpa's outhouse when I visited his farm. Every time I was on my way to the outhouse he would always say, "Don't use the shiny pages in the catalog." I thought he wanted to keep the best pages for himself. One day I felt a little more rebellious than usual, so I used the shiny pages. It didn't take long to realize this was a big mistake. Much to my surprise the shiny pages were slippery, non-absorbent, and non-effective. I never used the shiny pages again. After this harsh experience, I listened more closely to grandpa's advice.

Merle wasn't home when I delivered his gift. But when he opened it he immediately found me and while laughing he declared, "That's the best gift I ever received. Thanks so much for the outhouse. I have a special place for it in my village." He displayed my gift in a special place in his town every Christmas.

Not everyone appreciated my gifts, and with a limited allowance I had to be inventive. One Christmas my brother and I went shopping and he spent all his money on a beautiful hand-painted meat platter for Mom. A turkey was painted in the middle and was surrounded with colorful flowers. He got more allowance than me since he was twenty-two months older, and I knew I couldn't afford to get Mom a nice present like his. However, I couldn't let my brother get a better present for Mom, so I searched the store until I came upon the perfect gift. It was a hand-painted picture on varnished wood. It cost a dollar (five months allowance) and I had enough money left over to buy Dad a tool since he was a carpenter. My brother didn't buy Dad anything since he spent all his money on Mom's present. Before Christmas we would give Mom hints about her gift. He bragged, "My gift is hand-painted." So I boasted "My gift is hand-painted too." On Christmas morning, Mom opened his gift first and marveled at the beauty of the platter. Then she opened mine and just about fell off the chair laughing. She showed our gifts to all our guests that Christmas. She showed his gift first and everyone marveled at the beauty of the platter and complimented him on how thoughtful he was for getting such a nice gift. Then she announced, "And this is what my daughter got me." When they saw my hand-painted picture they laughed until tears came to their eyes. I didn't understand what was so funny about the picture until years later when I bought a house. Mom presented me with my hand-painted varnished wooden picture as a house-warming gift. Now I understand why everyone laughed when they saw my Christmas present. The picture portrayed a lady dressed in a red improper outfit sitting on a curb with her stockings rolled down. Large black words at the top of the picture stated, "EVERYTHING I LIKE IS ILLEGAL, IMMORAL, OR FATTENING." I was just eight years old when I bought that picture, and I thought it was as nice as my brother's platter since it was hand-painted on varnished wood. Mom kept that picture all these years.

Maybe these stories were the first indicator that I was a cartoon character. As I continued to reflect, I started to see things a little clearer. I cringed when I remembered how I looked in my second grade picture. My hair was parted in the middle and pulled back in braids, my front teeth were missing, and I still wore gold thick wire-rim safety glasses that were always bent so half of one eye was above the glasses. I was a tomboy and always had skinned knees. I had to wear dresses to school. I hated that! I always managed to tear out the hem and rip the ties. I may not have been a cartoon character yet, but I certainly looked the part.

As I journeyed back to my early years in the forties, I remembered that little girls were expected to be dressed in flurry dresses, playing with dolls, and having tea parties; I was outside dressed in my brother's old jeans and flannel shirts, playing baseball, horseshoes, and climbing trees. I was loud and a bit obnoxious. My brother loved cowboys, so being the tomboy that I was; we played cowboys and Indians every day. I dressed in a cowboy outfit with a cowboy hat, cowboy boots with spurs, and to complete my outfit I buckled a holster to my waist and tied it to my leg. Our six shooters actually shot plastic bullets. My brother always had to be the good guy; therefore, I was always the bad guy, but I didn't mind. One day he wanted to be a horse, so I ran after him and lassoed him. I put the rope around his waist and followed him around the Wild West while holding onto the reins. After a while of rounding up the outlaws, I tied him to the gas pipe by the garage and went into the saloon for a sarsaparilla. While I was in the saloon, I heard my horse whinnying and figured he was trying to break away. I wasn't concerned since I had him tied securely to the pipe. However, I ran out of the saloon when the whinnying turned into wailing. When he reared up to run away the rope pulled him down and he hit his head on the edge of the sidewalk and split it open. I didn't understand why I got into trouble for this. He was my horse and I tied him to the post just like in the movies. It was his fault for trying to get away, not mine. I wasn't even there. I was inside the saloon sipping on a sarsaparilla. He was fine after a trip to the doctor's and a few stitches. He got ice cream. I didn't!

One hot summer afternoon I was sitting on the sofa talking to my aunt Esther. My nose was stuffed up and I tried everything to clear it out. Finally I put my finger on the right side of my nose and blew. A gigantic booger rocketed out of my nose and landed right on my brother's back. Did I mention he was shirtless? I saw that booger on his back at the same time he felt it. I took off and he was right behind me. He was yelling, "Wait till I get my hands on you!" I was screaming, "Help! Help!" My aunt intervened just as he caught me and was about to clobber me. She yelled, "Let her go!" He shouted, "She put a booger on my back!" My aunt bellowed, "It was an accident!" He roared, "No it wasn't. She did it on purpose!" Aunt Esther explained, "Now, how could she aim a booger from her nose so it would land on your back?" He shoved me and let me go. I think if my aunt wasn't there I wouldn't be here today.

Another time, my brother and I were alone in the car waiting for our parents to return from the bank; we decided to decorate the upholstery on the door with the cigarette lighter. The cigarette lighter was round and had a series of circles. We took turns to see who could make the prettiest design on the door. Our turn was up when the lighter cooled. Then we would plug the lighter into the socket and get it hot again. When Mom came back she didn't notice the beautiful designs on the door. She noticed the smell of scorched ruined upholstery. She wasn't too pleased. I couldn't figure out why she was so upset. I thought the door looked great. After being grounded for awhile, I realized we could have caught the car on fire and maybe we ruined the upholstery a little.

Mom and Dad had plans to go out one night. My brother and I were getting older and didn't think we needed a babysitter anymore. We stayed home alone in the daytime but never at night. We begged them to let us stay home alone. Reluctantly they finally agreed if we promised not to fight or get into trouble. We promised. We felt brave and enjoyed our new freedom. We explored the off-limit territory and ate a snack on the couch in the living room. For some mysterious reason food tasted better where we were forbidden to eat. While we were playing cards we heard a knocking on the side of the garage. The atmosphere suddenly became eerie. We froze waiting and listening to see if we heard the knock again. We did! We tried to figure out what was making the sound. We thought someone was knocking, but why were they constantly knocking on the side of the garage? Neither of us wanted to venture outside to see who or what was knocking. We were frightened and regretted being home alone. We bickered a little over whose idea it was to be left alone. Finally I climbed up on the kitchen sink and pulled up the blind and cautiously peeked out the window. The brisk wind wove through the trees and monstrous shadows lurked back and forth. The knocking continued and the fear made my skin tingle. I couldn't see the side of the garage where the knocking was coming from. Finally I couldn't stand the suspense of the knocking any longer, so despite my terror, I opened the window, stuck my head out, and looked in the direction of the noise. Much to my relief I discovered it was the extra rope of the clothesline hanging down and the wind was blowing it against the garage. This discovery was such a relief, and we became brave again.

Grandma gave Mom a rocker when she had another baby. It was an old-fashioned wooden rocker with long rockers in the back. One afternoon when my brother and I were home alone I got a brainstorm to have a contest to see who could rock the hardest without tipping over. We took turns rocking as hard as we could. It was a great thrill ride and balancing act. The contest was well under way and we each had four turns, and neither of us had tipped over yet. It was an art rocking so hard that you almost tip over and then gaining momentum and tipping the other way as far as you can. Everything was going well until one of us rocked too close to the couch and broke off one of the rockers. The good time was over now and we knew we were in big trouble. We feared being grounded for the rest of our lives and Dad's belt would surely come off. We argued about whose fault it was, but it didn't matter because from past experience we would both be punished. As ingenious as we were at the time, we came up with the idea of taping the rung back together with black electrical tape. Lucky for us the rocker was black. I held the broken rocker in place while my brother taped it together. After we were finished we rocked normal to see if the tape would hold it together. It did. You really had to look close to notice the black electrical tape. Later, when Mom was rocking my baby brother, we cringed and hoped the tape would hold. We both knew it was just a matter of time before we would be busted. Sure enough Mom caught on to us since we were acting guilty and kept looking at the electrical tape hoping it would hold together the broken part every time she rocked. One afternoon she discovered our handy work and asked, "Why is this electrical tape on here?" We confessed and she said, "I could have fallen with the baby." Needless to say we were put out of commission for a while and our allowances helped purchase a new rocker.

Most of my friends went to school with me so I suppose they have been observing my cartoony behavior as early as that. A few things come to mind that may be considered comical to an observer. When I was in the fourth grade I had the lead part in our Christmas play. I was the mother and my classmates were my husband and children. I was great at rehearsal. I spoke articulately and with expression. Everyone knew his lines and the performance was flawless at practice. On the day of the play our parents came, and when I peeked out of the curtain and saw them, nervousness I wasn't accustomed to overwhelmed me. I suddenly forgot my lines, and thought, "I can't do this!" I worked hard to curb my anticipation of failure. I took a deep breath and looked over my lines. Then I realized the play was about to begin, along with this realization came an upsurge of emotion quite like stage fright. My palms were sweating, there was a gnawing in the pit of my stomach, my knees were weak, my mouth was dry, and my heart was pounding. We took our places and the curtain opened. This was the first time we were dressed in our costumes. I felt a little silly dressed as a mother with clothes too big for me, and my classmates looked comical. When my classmates started to say their lines something overpowered me, and as I looked at them I started giggling. When it was my turn I could hardly speak from my giggling. Before long I had the whole cast giggling. It was a total disaster; the more I tried to compose myself, the harder I laughed. I couldn't explain the feeling that overcame me. After the play Mom told me, "I didn't come to see you laugh," and she often told the story of my début in this school play. Funny thing I was never asked to be in a school play again. Imagine that. That was my first and last performance!

The next year the teacher picked a group of us to draw a picture on the chalkboard for Thanksgiving. We were almost finished when she made a comment that it was not very colorful. So I started erasing the picture even though I felt the picture looked realistic. When the teacher noticed this she appeared annoyed and sent me to my seat. Bewildered, I went to my seat pondering why she was upset with me. She made a negative comment about the picture so I figured we should make our Thanksgiving picture more colorful. The group of artists at the chalkboard wasn't too happy with me either, since they had to start drawing from the beginning. I wasn't chosen for anymore artwork on the chalkboard.

I had a growth spurt over the summer of fifth grade, which led to my most embarrassing moment. My fifth grade teacher came into the classroom to talk to the sixth grade teacher, and I noticed them looking in my direction while they were talking. After a while the fifth grade teacher looked directly at me and commanded, "Stand up. My goodness how much you have grown over the summer!" Needless to say the boys had a field day with that announcement. It took all year to live her statement down.

Gosh my early years were tough. However, I was about to embark on a new journey of my life through the woods and over the river into the town of Sharpsville. The people there hadn't seen the little knock-kneed, pigeon-toed, pig-tailed, toothless tomboy with the bent glasses and torn dresses who was banned from plays and artwork. I was headed to junior high in the big town where no one knew my awkward stage.

I reckoned I needed to change some of my tomboyish behavior, so I decided to take baton, tap, ballet, and acrobat lessons. Thus, I replaced my bat with a baton, my cowboy boots and spurs for tap and ballet shoes, my flannel shirts and jeans for tutus and leotards. My tree climbing, baseball, and horseshoes days were over. The backyard was no longer the Wild West but a place for a tomboy to turn into a coordinated young lady. Now I danced around the yard twirling, leaping, bending, and gliding effortless through the air defying gravity.

Next my thick, gold, bent, wire-rim glasses were replaced with cool cat eye glasses. My braids were cut off, and my aunt gave me a home permanent. My legs and feet straightened so my knees didn't knock anymore and I was no longer pigeon-toed. The payday before school started, Mom took me to the top floor of the Murphy Store in downtown Sharon where I got fitted for my first bra. It was referred to as a training bra. I didn't know why and you didn't ask questions back in the day. Then Mom bought me two new poodle skirts, a slip with yards and yards of netting so my skirts stuck out and swished when I walked, two cardigans, and some scarves for around my neck. Then I went to the shoe department and bought my new saddle shoes and bobby socks. My friends and I decided we needed a clean slate in the new town and new school, so we all broke up with our boyfriends.

On the first day of school I put on my cool gray skirt with a pink poodle on the front and my netted slip which made my skirt flare out. I wore a pink cardigan backwards and tied a pink scarf around my neck. Next I put on my bobby socks and laced up my saddle shoes. I combed my newly permanent waved hair and put on my cat eye glasses. Now I was ready to embark on the next phase of my life.

I went to my friend's house and we walked to the bus stop where I eagerly waited for the bus. She was a year older than me and was amused by my excitement. Finally the bus came and drove me through the woods and over the river into the town of Sharpsville where I would attend Junior High. Well it didn't take long for my bubble to burst. The town people referred to us as farmers, which didn't make sense since just a few of us lived on farms. I soon realized the fresh variety of city slicker boys to choose from in Junior High weren't much different from the farmers. However, on my way to the school bus one afternoon a certain patrol boy caught my eye and I thought, "Wow, is he cool. Could this be my prince charming?" The patrol boy's name was Tom. I didn't know it at the time but I was baptized on the same day he was born. This surely was a sign we were destined to get together.

I didn't actually meet Tom until eighth grade music class. We were drawn to each other because we had something in common; we were the only students in the class with absolutely no talent or interest in the modus operandi of music. We had no desire to play a musical instrument or sing. The only music I was interested in was Pat Boone and Elvis singing on my 33 records. However, the class was mandatory! I tried to pay attention in class, but I didn't understand a thing the teacher was talking about. Whole notes, half notes, and quarter notes, the only notes I knew or cared about were the notes I passed to my friends.

One day the music instructor announced that everyone had to try out for choir. So he lined us all up in the hallway in front of this small room where they stored music equipment. He called out our names one at a time to audition whether we wanted to or not. I felt like I was lined up for a firing squad. When my name was called, off I went like a tuba among the violins. I immediately felt overwhelmed when I saw musical instruments everywhere and the music stands had papers with marks that looked somewhat like hieroglyphics written all over them. I felt like I was crossing the threshold into another world. I cautiously walked around the instruments over to the piano where the teacher was seated and he demanded, "Sing the scale forward and backward." I knew how to do this because he made us sing this in every class. So he started to play the piano and I proceeded to sing, "Do, re, me, fa, so, la, te, do, do" He yelled, "Stop! Stop! Next!" I thought, "How rude!" Tom had a similar experience. However, he only got to sing, "do, re, me" before the teacher yelled, "Stop! Stop! Next! I don't know how we passed that class.

As I continued my journey down memory lane some of my friends witnessed my first driving experiences down the looney tooney road. I took drivers training in high school; the first semester we learned the rules of the road from the text book and the second semester we drove a real car. I remember the first time I got behind the wheel. The teacher drove us to a deserted road, pulled over, and told me to get behind the wheel. I did and then started the car. I slowly drove to the end of the road and started to turn right toward a field. He stated, "Turn left." I continued turning right toward the field. He shouted, "Turn left! Left!" I continued to turn right heading straight into the field thinking he got mixed up and said left instead of right. Then he grabbed the wheel and turned it left. I stopped the car and looked at him and asked, "Do you want me to drive on the road?" He looked at me and bellowed, "Yes!" I couldn't believe he wanted me to drive on the actual road with real cars. I had never been behind the wheel of a car before. How could I drive on the real road where real cars traveled? Well much to my surprise, I did. I drove for twenty minutes and was amazed at how well I drove. However I had to live with the comments from the backseat drivers, "Don't you know your left from your right? Is that where you farmers drive, in the field?" It didn't take them long to spread the rumor of my first driving experience around.

Next were lessons from my brother. I stopped at a stop sign and I looked up and down and up and down and up and down the street to see if a car was coming. Finally he asked, "What are you doing; waiting for a car to come." I just couldn't muster the courage to go. I feared a car would start down the street while I was looking up the street or a car would start up the street while I was looking down the street. Eventually I gunned the car and bolted across the street before any cars came into view. I still hesitate at intersections.

The teacher took us to a wide street by the football field where there was plenty of room to practice turning around. He advised, "Be sure to go to the test area and practice before you take your driving test because it's much smaller." I didn't! I flunked! It didn't take long for this to get around school, and the stories about driving in the field surfaced again. The next day I went to the area and practiced. The next week I passed my driving test.

Shortly after I got my license my aunt came for a visit. My cousin, Nancy, forgot something at her house and wanted me to take her to get it. The only problem was Dad had the car. My aunt offered her car. Just one minor detail: her car was a standard-shift and I never drove a standard-shift car. I could hardly drive an automatic car. Nancy pleaded, "Come on, I know how to work the gears and you can do the pedals." My aunt explained the process of driving with the gears and pedals. When I understood the process, we practiced in the driveway: I at the pedals and Nancy at the gears. We performed our shared duties and after a couple of false starts the car moved. It was jerk, jerk, abrupt stop then chug, chug, zoom. We headed for the road after we perfected our duo shift and when the chug, chug, zoom outnumbered the jerk, jerk abrupt stops.

I was fine as long as I didn't have to stop. When we approached a stop sign, I told Nancy to look for cars and if no cars were coming I didn't stop. (Back in the day people only had one car and there wasn't much traffic on the country roads). We almost made it to her house without stopping, but I had to stop just before turning onto her road. When we started performing our duo we were back to jerk, jerk abrupt stops. After a few of these, a neighbor of hers apparently observed our predicament and started toward the car. He was a few feet from the car when we kicked into chug, chug, zoom and away we went. Nancy waved as we zoomed to her house. She ran into her house and got her stuff. When she returned we started the same process, only in the opposite direction. It's incredible we made it home. Our guardian angels were surely working overtime. I stayed away from standard-shift cars after that experience.

Around this time Tom and my friendship shifted toward a more serious romantic relationship, so we exchanged class rings and started going steady. I never noticed any of his bizarre Lally Logic during our courtship. On our journey through dating we were inseparable, enjoying the same things and doing everything together as though we were one person. We went to the homecomings, proms, movies, dinner, shopping, for long walks, and talked for hours. He was so interested in everything I had to say. Of course every so often we would go our separate ways, but sooner or later we would get back together. It was as though he was a magnet and I was steel, he was the bread and I was the butter.

Tom played football, and after the games he would walk me home. We would discuss everything; we never ran out of things to talk about. When we were together he made me feel like I was the most important person in the world. It was the best time of our lives, and we were deliriously happy.

We hung out at a fast food restaurant with our classmates, but our favorite place to go for burgers was a place called "The Burp." After we ate our burgers and fries Tom would look into my eyes and tenderly say, "We are at The Burp so I have to burp." Then he would open his mouth wide and let out a long loud burp. After that, we laughed hysterically. I thought he was so clever and adorable.

One of our favorite places to go was the drive-in theater. Periodically Tom would drive off from the parking place with the speaker still in the window. He would have to back up and put the speaker on the pole. Sometimes he pulled the cord from the pole. We would giggle while making a quick get-a-way before the manager noticed. We felt a bit like Bonnie and Clyde.

The best joke I ever heard was the one I was told as a teen about the drive-in theater. The joke: "Did you hear about the couple who froze to death at the drive-in? No, what happened? They went to see "Closed for the Winter!" I laughed so hard the first time I heard that joke. I could just picture a couple sitting in their car waiting for the movie to start. Every time I went past a drive-in theater in the winter and saw "CLOSED FOR THE WINTER" posted on the billboard, I laughed out loud. To this day when I think of this joke, I giggle.

The teachers also noticed the change in our friendship. One day Tom was dozing off in class and the history teacher jokingly asked me, "Are you keeping Tom up too late?" The teacher in typing class moved him so he couldn't sabotage my typewriter. He would push a button on my typewriter and I couldn't type until the ribbon rewound. He would walk by and bump my chair and try to mess up my typing. He was so adorable. When Tom wasn't in my class he was always waiting outside the door of my classroom to walk me to my next class, even though he may be late for his class.

One afternoon an announcement came over the speakers, "Attention: All seniors who have talent of any kind are welcome to perform in the senior talent show scheduled for class day. All interested seniors meet in the auditorium for rehearsal after school on Friday." My friend and I got caught up in the moment and decided to do a tap dance we had preformed in a recital when we were thirteen. We put on our shocking pink leotard, black netted gloves, black netted hose, high heel tap shoes, and attached our white feather onto our hair. Our outfits had been in storage for the past five years. Lucky for us we matured early and were the same size as we were at age thirteen, so off we went in our outfits to the auditorium for rehearsal. We both regretted this decision shortly after we entered the auditorium that Friday; especially after we performed our dance for the other students at the talent rehearsal. What were we thinking? Somehow it wasn't as much fun tapping when you are a cool, almost eighteen-year-old teenager as it was when you were thirteen. What a disastrous way to end your senior year. We made a conscious decision not to go back. However the teacher in charge insisted we return.

We fretted about our dilemma for the next couple of days. Then the unexpected happened. After gym class we were racing up the stairs to the girls' locker room and she ran into the door and broke her toe. We were concerned about her injury until we realized that she couldn't tap dance. We both jumped for joy, and later that day we went and told the teacher we couldn't perform in the talent show.

On class day, as we sat and watched the talent show, our hearts went out to some of our classmates who performed. Not the ones with talent but the ones like us who got caught up in the moment and committed to performing. The act that sticks in my mind to this day is the group who sang "Lollipop." Their outfits were hilarious. They wore short frilly little girl dresses and held a large lollipop while swaying from side to side as they sang. It was disastrous and everyone laughed. Then I thought of how hilarious we would have looked stomping, toe, heeling, brush, and ball changing in our shocking pink leotard, black netted gloves, black netted hose, high heel tap shoes, and a feather attached to our hair. The broken toe saved us from this dreadful humiliation.

As I looked back at some of my adventures growing up maybe there was a hint of a cartoon character forming in the little knocked-kneed tomboy with braids and bent glasses. How could I be any other character running around the neighborhood dressed like a cowboy on my quest to tame the Wild West. Without a doubt the rocking chair contest, the flying booger, and the cigarette lighter art were adventures straight out of a comic strip. My debut as an actor, artist, singer, and dancer was a once in a lifetime performance. (I was only asked once) After graduation Tom entered the Air Force and I went to work at General Motors. We married in 1964. Now I had a partner. However, I didn't know at the time that I had a partner in the "Looney Tunes."

2

Liz The Cartoon Character

After reminiscing over my early years, it was becoming clearer why my friends defined me as a cartoon character, so I continued to journey back in time and discovered I occasionally wandered onto the looney tune trail. I was amazed at all the cartoony stories that came to my mind that I never looked at in that way before.

The first one happened shortly after we purchased our house. I bought a pair of doves that looked great on my coffee table. They were expensive for knickknacks, but I rationalized they would be a good investment since I really liked them and would keep them on my coffee table *forever*. I dusted my precious doves with a cloth weekly and once a month I would immerse them into water to remove the built up dust. After a while, I noticed my doves were slowly disintegrating. I wondered, "What is happening to my treasured doves?"

One afternoon a friend noticed too. By now I had a pair of white unrecognizable clumps. She examined my doves and informed me, "Your doves are made of alabaster. You should never use water to clean them." I thought, "You shouldn't clean a knickknack with water. That doesn't make sense." I asked her, "Then how do you clean them?" She answered, "I don't know. I just heard that you should never use water on alabaster." After she left, I researched alabaster and discovered this: "Most people don't realize that water is the biggest enemy of alabaster and can ruin the appearance of the soft stone. Instead, dust your knickknacks and carvings made of alabaster regularly with a soft cloth. AVOID USING WATER."

After reading this I thought, "Really, I always use a soft cloth; I never heard of a hard cloth." It is *impossible* to dust a *white* knickknack with a soft cloth in a house with three children. Why would someone make a knickknack out of this material? WHY? I ASK, "WHY?" In my wildest dreams I would not have thought that a knickknack would have been made from a disintegrating material. Where are my expensive doves that were to sit on my coffee table *forever*? From this day forward I never bought anything without knowing exactly what it was made from; I never bought anything made of alabaster again!

Shortly after this I went to a pottery store to find something cheap to replace my treasured doves that were expensive and didn't last forever. I picked up a picture frame, examined it, and put it back on the shelf. Zoom, just like dominoes, all the frames fell backward and knocked all the vases off the shelf behind it onto the floor. The crash was thunderous. All the vases broke. I stood in disbelief as people came from all around to see what and who caused the loud crash. Thank goodness the employee that was the first on the scene was perturbed at the way the items were displayed. She told me, "This wasn't your fault. I knew those frames would fall sooner or later, but no one would listen to me. This was a disaster waiting to happen." I slipped away while she was complaining and cleaning up the mess I set in motion.

The mailman delivered a free sample of deodorant one afternoon while I was getting ready to meet my friend for lunch. I sprayed some under my arms and went on my way. While I was at lunch I noticed my underarms felt a little sticky and itchy. Apparently my underarms were sensitive to the new deodorant.

Halfway through lunch my friend told me about a free sample she received in the mail. She said, "All you do is spray it into your dryer to reduce static cling." Instantly, I thought about the free sample that arrived in the mail that morning and my sticky, itchy underarms. Could I have mistaken the static cling spray for deodorant? I asked her, "What is the name of the static cling spray?" And sure enough it was the same name as the deodorant I sprayed under my arms earlier. I couldn't bring myself to tell my friend I also got a free sample in the mail with the same name and sprayed it under my arms. One of us was wrong about the product. And I was hoping it wasn't me. By the time I arrived home my underarms were very irritated. I checked the free sample and the words

"SPRAY IN YOUR DRYER TO ELIMINATE STATIC CLING" were printed on the label in big red letters. I totally overlooked the words "spray in your dryer" and interpreted "eliminate static cling" as a deodorant that prevents static in your clothes so they don't stick to your underarms. The good that came out of this experience is I read labels very carefully from that day forward.

I continued down that confusion trail and found more evidence of my comical behavior. For some mysterious reason, daylight savings time has always confused me. Over the years, I have lost count of all the times I forgot to set the clock ahead or back an hour; therefore, I have experienced every possible scenario of being early or late for appointments. The worst situation is when I'm an hour late for church. Clueless I walk down the aisle looking for a seat totally unaware that mass is nearly over. I have to walk to the front of the church because for some reason unknown to me the seats fill up in the back of the church first. I finally find a seat and a short time later everyone stands and the priest starts to recite the closing prayer, which I assume is the opening prayer. Sometime during the closing prayer I become aware that it's not the opening prayer and then I realize its daylight savings time and I am an hour late for mass. I cringe of embarrassment as the priest says, "The mass is over go in peace." I guess this is an ongoing thing I will have to deal with for the rest of my life.

Likewise, when it comes to directions I have no sense. We were on our way to our daughter's basketball game and couldn't find the school in Oil City. We drove around the town several times. After much pleading from me and the realization that the game was about to start, Tom finally stopped at a gas station and said, "Okay go in and get directions to the school." I went into the gas station and asked for directions. I repeated them to Tom and he drove down the street and made a left then a right. We were cruising along when he suddenly slammed on the brakes. He stopped just inches from the river. We were on a boat ramp. He knows I am the worst navigator and shouldn't have sent me for directions. He drove around a while longer looking for the school and then drove home. We are a pathetic pair! Tom won't ask for directions and I can't follow them. It's a wonder we get anywhere. Later I discovered the game wasn't in Oil City. It was a home game!

Sometimes I respond to my observations and they aren't always as I perceive. A while back my daughter and I went to a restaurant for lunch. We had to wait for a table so we started toward the seats in the lobby to wait to be seated. A couple of ladies approached the seats at the same time. I glanced at one lady and said, "You go ahead and sit because you are pregnant." She shouted, "I am not pregnant!" I apologized, "Oh, I'm sorry but you look AAAH, you have on, oh, I'm sorry." Then we all stood beside the empty seats. No one sat down. It was difficult to keep my composure as I tried to act nonchalantly and not make eye contact with her. I couldn't help thinking, "Why in the world do women wear blouses that look like maternity tops."

A while back we attended the wedding of a friend's daughter. The bride and groom were both teachers on an Indian reservation in Oklahoma. The bride was beautiful and the wedding was memorable. While we were at the reception I noticed the bride and bridal party dancing. They were all dancing the same steps and moved together with the same arm and hand movements. The song sounded like an Indian song, and the dance rhythm reminded me of an Indian dance. Since the bride and groom taught on an Indian reservation I thought, "How sweet, she taught her friends an Indian dance and they are all dancing it together on her wedding day." Thank goodness I thought this and did not speak it out loud. Weeks later I discovered the song was not an Indian song. It was the Macarena.

We took a family vacation to Florida and stopped in Miami to visit Tom's aunt. In the evening we went to the dog races. It was crowded and we had to park in the back of the parking lot, which was full of sand. It was very difficult to walk and after a while of sinking into the sand I got a little perturbed and complained in the crowded lot, "Why in the world would they haul all this sand into a parking lot?" I noticed people around me snicker. Tom then informed me, "This is Florida; there is sand everywhere." I knew that.

When I took classes at Penn State a classmate was transferring to Edinboro University. My daughter went to school there and the winters were very treacherous; she often said she would slip and slide to class. So I told him to be careful he doesn't fall in the winter because the weather there is wicked. He was in a wheelchair."

Tom and I attended a dinner with some of our friends. I went to the ladies room and discovered a lady who was quite upset. Everyone tried to console her. Apparently she had an argument with her husband on the way to the dinner. When I finally came back to the table, Tom asked, "What took so long?" I proceeded to tell him about the upset lady in the restroom who had a fight with her husband and how we had tried to console her. A while later, the disturbed lady came from the restroom and sat down next to the fellow sitting on the other side of me."

I continued journeying back in time and noticed I occasionally took a detour down the looney tune trail as a volunteer. I was fortunate to be a stay-at-home mom, so I had plenty of time to volunteer for many organizations. I became a Girl Scout Leader, not by choice but as the result of attending a meeting. Our daughter, Maureen, was in second grade and brought home a note inviting her to join Girl Scouts; she was really excited. I went to the meeting and much to my surprise only four mothers came. The lady in charge looked at us and announced, "If there is going to be a Girl Scout Troop and Brownie Troop, you are the leaders." Then she pointed to me and another lady and said, "You two ladies are the Brownie Leaders" and then pointed to the two other ladies and said, "You are the Girl Scout Leaders." We were all shocked by this statement. We pondered over this realization and came to the conclusion that if we didn't accept the challenge we would be going home to disappointed little girls. Reluctantly, we accepted the leadership. I went to a meeting to join my daughter into scouting and came home a Scout Leader.

I attended trainings and learned the in and outs of running a Brownie troop. We performed flag ceremonies, made crafts, sang songs, worked on badges and carried out community projects. The meetings were running smoothly. However, every so often I would wander down that scouting looney tune trail. At the Brownie meetings I noticed the girls moving away from me when we were singing. I thought this a little peculiar, until one day I felt a tap on my shoulder and one of the girls asked, "Mrs. Lally, would you please stop singing? You are messing us up!"

The next year, due to the large number of girls signing up for Brownies, we divided into two troops. One troop met on Monday, and my troop met on Friday. We decided to plant tulips as a service project to show our appreciation to the school for letting us have our meetings there. The janitor dug an area for us to plant our bulbs. We divided the area in half with an imaginary line, and one troop planted their bulbs on Monday and we planted our bulbs on Friday of the same week. In the spring the tulips only came up on one half of the flower bed, and it wasn't ours. What are the odds of not one bulb growing? The bulbs came from the same package and were planted in the same soil. The only thing that wasn't the same was *me*! Did I perhaps instruct the girls to plant the bulbs in the same place as the other troop?

I strolled on that looney tune trail right from the start when I took the Brownies camping in the afternoon. The camp director told us to pick an area and set up our camp. We explored the campgrounds and picked an area under a shade tree. We went to the tool shed and got a tent, mallets, and other supplies we needed. The girls worked diligently for about an hour, and finally our camp was ready for inspection. After the camp director inspected our camp site, she informed me, "You will have to move your campsite. You pitched your tent over poison ivy!" All the girls scrubbed their exposed parts.

Our project for the day was to make a terrarium from the wild plants around the camp. I took the girls on a hike through the woods to gathered plants. Then we went into the cabin and assembled our terrarium and put it on the display table with the other terrariums. Later, the camp director privately informed me that our terrarium had poison ivy and weeds in it not plants. Again all the girls scrubbed their exposed parts. The positive outcome was my scouts learned to recognize poison ivy in one afternoon.

The next summer, we went hiking into the woods and saw some large beautiful plants growing on a hillside. The girls wanted to climb the hill and get a closer look at the plants. I told the girls to go and stand by the plants so I could take a group picture. While the girls were climbing the hill they started complaining, "Something stinks up here. What is that terrible smell?" When they got near the plants the ground was soft and their feet sunk up to their ankles. I snapped their picture even though they were complaining about the smell and were tripping on the plants and soft dirt. Later the camp director informed me that the beautiful plants they posed in were *skunk cabbage*.

At the end of third grade we had a special ceremony and the Brownies became Girl Scouts and I became a Girl Scout Leader. This move involved more training, and the projects were more complex. Singing was still an issue and camping was now overnight, which led to more opportunities to stroll down the scouting looney tune trail.

We took the girls camping for a weekend in the fall, and most of the girls wanted to sleep outside in tents. We separated the girls into groups of four per tent, and they pitched their tents all around the field. We ended the day roasting marshmallows, singing, and telling ghost stories around the campfire. Then the girls went to their tents to retire for the night. Strange thing, two of their tents were missing. This spooked the girls so everyone collected their gear and headed for the cabin. The girls snuggled around the fireplace while we called the police to report the missing tents. They felt safe in the cabin so they started telling ghost stories again. They were telling a story about a little girl who was home alone. She heard a knock on the door and when she answered it, there was a ghost who wore a large hat. Just then there was a knock on our cabin door. Instantly the girls got quiet and all eyes were on the door. I slowly opened the door and there stood a state trooper wearing a large hat. The girls took one look at him, screamed, and ran into the next room. He had already found the tents in the ditch by the road. Apparently, some of the boys in the area got a kick out of annoying the Girl Scouts when they came to the camp and were always pulling pranks.

The next year we arrived Friday night at the camp, and the girls were eager to work on their camping badges. They really roughed it and existed with little comforts. They made campfires, hiked in the woods, slept in tents, and used an out-house. They carried water from an outside pump, so bathing was not high on the list. Everyone smelled like a campfire, and a couple of the girls tore their jackets and jeans while hiking through the woods. Sunday, we rode to church on the back of a hay wagon. At the beginning of mass the priest announced, "I would like to welcome the Girl Scouts from camp." Everyone looked in our direction. Later the girls asked, "How did they know we were the campers?" I looked at the other leaders and smiled.

About the time Maureen moved on to basketball, our daughter, Lora, joined Brownies. I started the cycle all over again and sometimes I ventured down the scouting looney tune trail with her troop. When Lora moved on to basketball our son, Marty, joined the Boy Scouts, so I became a den mother.

Each week, six cub scouts and another den mother met in my home. We worked on individual projects, and once a month we met with the Cub Scout Master and other dens. One Saturday we were going on an outing and I was sitting on a bus with the other den mothers waiting for the troop master. Since this was our first trip, he wanted to explain exactly where we were going and what he expected us to accomplish before the boys arrived. The troop master entered the bus and stood directly in front of me. I couldn't help but notice that the zipper on his pants was down, since it was eye level and all I could see when I looked up. It was hard to concentrate on what he was saying. I tried to raise my head and look at him, but I couldn't keep a straight face. So I looked straight ahead and all I could see was his unzipped fly. I didn't hear a word he uttered, given that I was fretting over if I should just pretend I didn't notice or if I should tell him. I felt I should tell him, but how could I interrupt a Cub Scout Master who I barely knew that was explaining the schedule of the day to a group of den mothers that his fly was open? I pondered over exactly what to say to him. I have told many men over the years their fly was down in unconventional ways, but I never told a stranger. I couldn't find the words to tell him, so I didn't. When he finished his talk, he got off the bus to get the boys.

When he came back inside the bus, his fly was zipped. Then I wondered, "Who told him and how did they tell him or did he discover it himself?" After looking around at the boys in the bus, I'm sure one of them told him in a quirky way. Then I wondered exactly where are we going and what am I expected to accomplish with my group of boys and which group of boys are under my supervision. I didn't hear a word the troop master uttered.

One morning I received a call from the religious education director at church who asked me to teach the sixth grade. Apparently, they didn't have a teacher for my daughter's class, and when the director asked if anyone knew of someone who would teach the class Lora volunteered me. I told the director I didn't feel qualified to teach religious education. She explained I would receive a teacher's manual that was very informative and there were religious classes for teachers I could attend. I accepted the challenge and taught classes for ten years. It was very rewarding. There weren't any cartoony experiences here. However, one day when I was in the church office talking to the director, the secretary asked me if I would help her once a week with odd jobs around the office such as stuffing envelopes and making copies. This was where I strolled down that looney tune trail, especially while using the copier when the priest was around.

For some reason I always feel uneasy and nervous around priests. I am overcome with this sensation that I should be holy or something. You know how it is sometimes when you haven't done anything wrong, but you feel guilty as if you might have. That is how I felt with the priest.

When the priest came into the copying room to chat, I was doomed. I would always mess up what I was copying. I always managed to bump the button and would shrink or enlarge what I was copying. I didn't discover it until well after he left, and many copies were ruined and had to be thrown out. I carried a large purse so I could dispose of my mistakes. I felt a little guilty about wasting the paper, so periodically I would anonymously put $20.00 into the collection to pay for the paper I wasted.

When I was winding down my volunteer work and considered taking classes at Youngstown University, I found myself in the most bizarre volunteer situation. I decided to look for a job near the campus and take some classes around my work schedule. I applied for a job at an old folks' home near the University. Shortly into the interview, I realized my job would be to fire the volunteers. Apparently, the volunteers and the staff didn't get along and weren't working together. This caused much chaos. Their problem was the volunteers were very influential people in the community and major contributors to the home. The directors didn't want to cause problems by asking them to leave. So my job description was fire the influential volunteers, find new volunteers to replace them, and build a rapport between the new volunteers and staff. It wasn't hard to figure out that I was going to be the scapegoat. I had a vision of the influential volunteers complaining to the director. She would blame me and say something to the effect, "I will look into it." Meanwhile, new volunteers would be set in place. Then I would be eliminated. I wasn't interested in the job after this realization, and besides, I didn't think I would be able to fire volunteers, especially since I had been a volunteer for most of my life.

I was an easy target as I traveled down the salesmen trail, and my associations with salesmen were definitely cartoony. Just like the comic strip characters, I was a sucker for any salesmen that came to my door or called on the phone. I always felt sorry for them and sensed an uncontrollable need for the product, and as a result I would buy anything they were selling whether I needed it or not. Before I was engaged I bought monogrammed linens, stainless steel pans, and a crystal rosary from door-to-door salesmen. I guess I bought the rosary to pray that I married a fellow with the initials I chose to put on my monogrammed linens. The stainless steel pots and pans could be used to whack the lucky fellow over the head to keep him in line.

I recall purchasing magazines over the phone. It was a one-time offer and just sounded too good to refuse. The fellow alleged, "We have a special offer to introduce you to our magazines. All you have to do is select six magazines and they will be sent to you absolutely free. This offer is just for today." Of course, I jumped at the offer. He explained, "You will receive a form in the mail and all you have to do is select your magazines and return the form in the enclosed envelope." I couldn't wait until Tom got home from work to tell him my good news. He just gazed at me and replied, "Nothing is free." Then he proceeded to remind me of all my past endeavors.

A few days later, I received my form in the mail, chose my magazines, mailed the form, and eagerly waited for their arrival. A couple of weeks later, I was shocked when Tom confronted me with a $90.00 bill for my free magazines (Darn! He's never home when the mail is delivered and why would he get the mail when I got this $90 bill for my *free* magazines). He read a copy of the form I filled out, and in small letters at the bottom of the page it stated, "These magazines are not free." I couldn't believe that salesman flat out lied to me. Ninety dollars was a lot of money in 1967 with minimum wage being ninety-nine cents.

I knew I would never hear the end of my *free* magazines especially when my six *free* magazines started coming in the mail as a reminder. I had to come up with a strategy of paying for the magazines. After much thought, a plan flashed through my mind; I rationalized that I would pay for the magazines with the money I saved by using the coupons. Back in the day, all the magazines had tons of really good coupons. He reluctantly bought my proposal and only occasionally brought up the subject of the magazines. However, he did say, "Nothing is free! I hope you learned a lesson." I didn't!

Another salesman came to the door and showed me a catalog listing items he was selling. As I was browsing through the catalog I noticed an ironing board cover which I needed so I ordered it. The salesman kept asking me what foods I liked and wouldn't leave. Since he had an accent it was hard for me to understand what he was saying. Finally he asked something I understood, "Doe yo lik a la pez za?" I answered, "Yes." Then he left. Boy was I surprised a week later when he delivered me frozen pizzas. I said, "There must be a mistake. I ordered an ironing board cover." He showed me the catalog again and started explaining in his broken English, and after a while I came to the realization that apparently the catalog items were what you received with the points you earned when you purchased the food. I paid for the pizza's and said, "No more!"

Salesmen continued knocking on my door and I continued buying whatever they peddled. While wandering down the looney tune trail with salesman, I bought wrapping paper, assorted cards, jewelry, clothes, cleaning products, candles, candy, popcorn, nuts, candy bars, cookies, hoagies and pies. It got to the point that I bought anything from anyone who came to the door. Tom made a comment, "You would buy crap if they tied a bow on it." I regret to admit that he was probably right.

Then one day while watching television I discovered a segment which revealed tactics that salesman use to entice people into buying their products. They are trained to use trickery and manipulation to take advantage of people. First they have a gimmick to get into your house with the idea once inside it will be harder for you to refuse them. Then they start their double talk and won't take no for an answer. They just continue to bring up another reason why you should buy their product. They intimidate and threaten you with their comments, "This is the last day to take advantage of this offer; you will never be offered this again. I am going to write your name down on this list." They tug at your emotions and wear you down.

After watching that program I felt angry, strong, and determined that no salesman would ever take advantage of me again. I planned a strategy for dealing with salesmen. I started locking the storm door and would talk through the glass. I shouted, "If you are a salesman, I don't want anything. *Goodbye!*" Then I shut the main door and did a victory dance.

Of course I would never turn away a child; I always support the local children in their fundraisers for their activities. I have enough Christmas wrapping and holiday cards to last me an eternity. Children were the only exception.

As I strolled on, I realized I was forced onto the looney tune trail by many circumstances that were out of my control. A few stories come to mind where I am the victim when I am forced into situations where the outcome is nothing but cartoony to an observer. For example I went to a local restaurant and ordered lemonade. The waitress asked, "What kind of lemonade do you want?" I answered, "Lemonade." She asked, "What flavor?" I replied, "Lemonade." She continued, "We have raspberry lemonade, pink lemonade, and strawberry lemonade." I responded, "I want lemon lemonade; just regular lemonade." If it's raspberry and pink it's not lemonade. Lemonade is made with lemons.

One summer I was planning a birthday party for my granddaughter. She picked a local fast food restaurant for her birthday lunch. I took everyone's order and off I went to pick up the food. I waited patiently in line and when it was my turn I said,

"I want eight children's meals." The clerk interrupted my order saying, "You can only have five children meals." I asked, "What?" She repeated, "You can only order five children meals?" I inquired "Why?" She explained, "Because they have Beanie Babies in them and you can only order five meals." I replied, "That doesn't make sense. Let me talk to the manager." The manager came over and I repeated my order and she responded, "You can only have five children meals." Again I asked, "Why?" She explained, "They have Beanie Babies in them and they have become so valuable people have been buying the meals just to get the Beanie Babies as a collector item. So we made a policy of only five children meals to a customer." I answered back, "Well I have a little birthday girl who picked your restaurant for her birthday lunch and she is excitedly waiting for her lunch along with seven of her playmates at my house. Now you tell me which three of these little ones don't get a children's meal?" She apologized, "I'm sorry, but that is our policy." So I stated, "If Beanie Babies are so valuable why in the world would you put them into a children's meal? It just doesn't make sense!" She confirmed, "I'm sorry I can only give you five children's meals." I continued, "You know I can get five children's meals here and go up the street and get the other three meals so why don't you just save me a trip and give me the eight meals." She answered, "I know." By this time a line was forming behind me and I felt like I was in a comic strip and any moment reality would set in and I would be on my way to the birthday party with my eight children meals.

As I stood there thinking about how stupid this policy was, an uncontrollable force overcame me and I was not going home without eight children's meals. Then I demanded, "Get your boss! I need to talk to him." Now she realized I wasn't going to leave without my eight children meals and I don't think she wanted to bother the boss so she rudely instructed the employee, "Give her the eight children's meals." She acted like she was doing me a favor. I didn't react to her rudeness because my thoughts were on the little ones at home who would finally get their birthday lunch. I thanked the lady and went on my way. I just don't understand why a fast food restaurant would put a valuable collectable into a children's meal and limit the meals for little children. That just doesn't make sense. A solution would be put the Beanie Babies into a collector's meal and limit the collector meals and put a toy into the children's meals.

There was a time when I had three children playing basketball. Going to all the games brought out the worst in me, and I found myself dribbling down the cartoon trail. At one game the other team played rough and dirty. The referees were letting them get away with elbowing our girls in the ribs, traveling, and letting them stand under their basket area for more than three seconds. Now I admit I don't know that much about the rules of basketball and miss most of the mistakes in the game. However, when I see the players' mistakes, they are certainly obvious. Something slowly overcame me and I found myself shouting at the referees and pointing out all their bad calls and mistakes. Apparently, I got carried away because one of the referees came over to me and handed me his whistle and asked, "Here do you want to referee the game?" What bothered me the most was that I pondered over what he asked and almost took the whistle out of his hand.

After the game we took Lora to the emergency room for X-rays since she was bent over in so much pain. She had badly bruised ribs. After this game I decided I would just sit and be quiet and not get so involved in the games. While I was sitting composed at the next game, the referees weren't making fair calls again and my mother-in-law yelled at the referee, "Stop that big cow!" That's all it took to get me going again. I will definitely take the whistle if it is offered to me a second time.

It has already been established that I have zero talent where singing is concerned, and as hard as I try I can't escape singing. I constantly find myself in situations where I am expected to sing and this journey is definitely down the looney *tune* trail. People avoid me when I sing, so I only sing occasionally when the situation warrants. I was at a retreat weekend and at one point we were all gathered together around the altar and the priest asked us to sing hymns. I was with my best friend. You know the one friend in a million you find in a lifetime. She was also a very good singer. I whispered, "Watch when I start singing everyone around me will move away and before long I will be standing alone." She declared, "No, not here at the retreat." We started to sing and sure enough I noticed people move away from me. I turned to tell my friend about the people moving away from me and much to my surprise she wasn't there. I walked over to where she moved and declared, "See what I mean! You even moved." She explained, "Oh, I didn't move because of your singing. I just wanted to get closer so I could hear the music better." Now this is my very best friend. Once the priest stated, "You are lucky if you can find one true friend in a lifetime." She is that friend and she moved! I hope God stayed.

I always enjoyed singing, dancing, and twirling my baton for an audience when I was young. However, now I only perform when I am alone. My favorite song to perform is "I Am Woman" by Helen Reddy. The tape starts with the announcer introducing, "Ladies and gentleman, here is Helen Reddy." I make an entrance from the hall into the living room with my microphone in hand, bow to the audience and proceed to accompany Helen Reddy. For a brief time I am a performer like Helen Reddy, but in reality I am performing like the Cartoon Character Betty Boop.

My journey took me along the baking trail back to a time when I sat at the table and watched my grandmothers and mother bake. I was instructed in the art of baking without measuring cups or spoons. The words dash, splash, pinch, and handful were constantly used. They put in a dash of salt and a splash of vanilla. I watched closely as they reached into a container and scooped out a handful of flour, sugar, or cornmeal. They poured milk or whatever liquid they were using right from the container. Crisco or butter was scooped from the container with their fingers. They used their senses and knew how much of an ingredient to add by feeling, looking at the texture, or tasting the mixture. Everything they made came out perfect. I was in awe of their baking.

This skill I never inherited or acquired so I often ventured down the looney tune baking trail trying to make sense of the recipes. I'm pathetic when it comes to baking. I follow a recipe accurately and measure everything precisely, and it rarely comes out right. I can't tell when it's done baking. My main problem is interpreting the instructions. Many times when preparing a recipe, I will discover when I look back on the page for more ingredients that I used the ingredients from two different recipes. Sometimes when my cake doesn't turn out I back track my steps and discover I am on a different page than the cake I started baking. This has happened more than once.

One morning as Maureen headed out the door for school she yelled, "You have to bring a Texas sheet cake to school by 4:00 today for the card party." "What!" I in a panic screamed! "All the parents have to bake a Texas sheet cake for the party" she yelled as she ran out the door. Maureen's basketball team was having a card party as a fund-raiser. That I knew, but the part about me baking a Texas sheet cake for desert I didn't know. I never heard of a Texas sheet cake, so I called one of the mothers and complained about not getting a notice about the cake and she replied, "I knew about it for weeks. My cake is baked and cooling." I asked her for the recipe, proceeded to the store for the ingredients, and baked my Texas sheet cake. I took it to the school and dropped it off. After the card party, my cake was sent home with Maureen. Apparently the cake didn't look delicious since it wasn't touched. Why do people assume everyone can bake? I can't! Later, I found out icing was supposed to be on the cake and I didn't put any on mine. I followed the directions my friend gave me over the phone. I guess she assumed I knew to put icing on the cake. When it comes to baking I am in a foreign land with a language I don't understand. However I didn't think my cake turned out that bad until Marty and Tom wouldn't eat it either, so I threw it out. I guess the cake had a few more issues than missing icing. Oh well, just one more baking disaster to add to my list.

You would think I could make a pineapple upside-down cake. Just the name sounds like it was invented for bakers like me. However, try as I might, I cannot get the knack of it. When I flip it over it is never how it should be. The last time I baked one, when I flipped it over it flew across the counter and landed into a pile of pineapple and chunks of cake. I love pineapple upside down cake and I will keep trying until I bake one just like Mom used to bake.

On the bright side we never have to check our smoke alarms since I set them off regularly with my cooking and baking. I even set them off when I set the oven to automatic cleaning.

As I journey through the plant kingdom I venture off on two trails; one is the jungle and the other is the desert. There is no in between. Every spring I proceed to the local florists and purchase the fullest, hardiest plants and arrange them throughout the house. My house looks like a jungle. I give them plant food, fertilize, and talk to them. Within a week they show signs of wilting and start thinning out. Before long they crumble and die and my house looks like a desert. One summer Lora and I watched the last of the leaves fall from my plant on the patio. All that was left was a slender twig in a pot of soil even though I talked, watered, and fertilized it. I love plants so again I went to the florists and purchased another variety of hardy plants, but the cycle continues. I have a small fortune invested in plants.

When we moved into our house all of our neighbors were retired and had large bountiful gardens. They took pride in their gardens and worked in them from dawn to dusk. While growing up we always had a garden and even though I didn't inherit my dad's green thumb I decided to plant a garden. Tom came out and looked over my garden and complained, "Your rows are all crooked. Look at how perfectly straight the neighbor's rows are." Later a neighbor came over and praised my garden and said, "I am glad to see you planted a garden." I told him what Tom had said and he replied, "You just tell him you planned it that way so you can get more plants in a row." The old men from the neighborhood visited when I worked in my garden and they taught me many tips on gardening. I grew beans, peppers, onions, tomatoes, cucumbers, corn, zucchini, and pumpkins. My garden was always a success and I always got much bounty from my plants. I think they tended to my garden when I wasn't around because after they passed away and new people moved in my garden slowly wilted away.

I love white daisies, so every spring I venture to the greenhouse and pick out some daisies just like the ones that used to grow wild in the fields where I grew up. I always plant a cluster in a barrel at the end of the patio. One spring I went to a green house and picked out some beautiful white daisies. I planted them and in a couple of weeks I noticed my beautiful white daisies starting to turn pink. By the end of the month, all the daisies were pink. Why do people experiment with plants and mess with *"Mother Nature?"* A perfectly beautiful flower found growing wild in nature was turned into an ugly pink color? Roses are another beautiful flower with a beautiful aroma that was totally destroyed. Go to your local florists and smell the roses. Don't bother; there is no smell. They destroyed a famous saying, "Stop and smell the flowers." There is no smell.

This fall the most bizarre thing happened in my plant kingdom. Tom yelled from the living room, "Liz, the leaves from your plant are falling on the floor." Periodically, we would find leaves on the floor of the living room. This wouldn't have surprised me if the plant was real but it was an artificial plant!

I have always been told that everyone has a talent; however, I haven't found mine yet. As I journeyed along searching for my talent I roamed down the craft trail. It didn't take me long to discover that I'm not crafty. I wanted a fall flower centerpiece for my table and discovered the price to be a bit extreme since it consisted of a dish, a piece of foam, and some flowers stuck in the foam. I thought, "I could make it at half the price. How hard could it be to stick flowers into a piece of foam?" So I bought the dish, foam, and flowers. When I got home I started to assemble my centerpiece. I glued the foam in the dish then I started to assemble the flowers into the foam. Well the stems of the flowers bent and they stuck out all over. When I was done, it looked like a preschooler had made it. Now I had to go back to the store and purchase the expensive assembled centerpiece.

My friend and I joined a craft of the month club and the first of every month we received a craft kit in the mail. When my kit arrived I assembled it with much difficulty, and it always came out crooked, bent, and uneven. I complained to my friend about the cheap parts and unclear directions. Then she showed me her perfectly assembled craft which she put together with ease. The result was always perfect for her. The craft kit that brought me to my knees was a three-tier candy dish. I followed the directions and baked the plastic in the oven and assembled my dish. The finished product was three melted plastic dishes on a crooked metal stick with a gob of melted plastic on top. I took my three-tier mess to my friend's house and was sure she would have similar trouble. But much to my surprise her candy dish was flawless and sitting on her table loaded with goodies. I don't understand how her crafts turn out perfect and mine turn out awful when we used the same kit and directions. I was committed to a year of crafts; however, instead of assembling craft of the month I assembled disaster of the month.

I decided to make a Christmas wreath with holly, bulbs, reindeer, and Santa; the end result was a big red velvet bow stuck on the bottom of the wreath. For Halloween I tried to assemble all kinds of spooky things on a wreath and eventually gave up and gave it to a friend to assemble for me. I got an urge to decorate a wreath for the fourth of July. I had the same terrible result and my wreath looked like something one would leave at a graveyard instead of put on the table for a celebration. I don't understand why I continue to be drawn to craft stores and have this overwhelming desire to make them when I haven't successfully completed one. I have quite a collection of craft supplies.

In spite of all this failure I still feel an uncontrollable desire to sing, even though people move away; grow plants, although their life span is short in my home; be creative and make crafts, even if not one has ever turned out, and bake, while the outcome is burned, under baked, and inedible.

I have driven many miles down the looney tune road over the years. Many times I feel like I'm driving the wrong way down a one-way street and people are shouting, "Get off the road." From time to time I feel I should have driven into that field the first time I got behind the wheel and stayed there, especially when Tom decided to economize and buy a standard-shift car to drive back and forth to work. This decision concerned me since I don't know how to drive a standard-shift car and economize is not in Tom's vocabulary. I haven't been behind the wheel of a standard-shift since I was sixteen when my cousin and I chugged to her house. He gave me two quick lessons and then I was on my own. He promised, "You will never have to drive the car since I will be driving it to work every day." Well the very next week when I went to the driveway to get into my car, the stick-shift car was there. I was mortified! I could hardly drive the car but I had to go to the store, so I decided to drive the car since there was only one stop sign on the way. Or I should say I chugged, zoomed, and came to an abrupt stop at the stop sign and the store. Then I made the mistake of parking on an incline and I couldn't back out of the parking space. After many false starts

I finally maneuvered out of that parking space with my jerking, chugging, zooming and then came to an abrupt stop at home. That day I taught myself how to drive the stick-shift in the driveway and at the end of our dead end street. I was not skilled at driving the stick-shift but I was better. Every time I started, I chugged, jerked and zoomed off. When I stopped, it was always an abrupt one.

That was just the start of him leaving me the standard-shift car. I never became skilled with that car; however, I always got where I was going. When I drove the children to school in the morning we would chug out of the driveway. Then I would drive along satisfactory until I had to stop for a stop sign. It was always an abrupt stop. Then I had to wait at the intersection until no cars were in sight so I could chug, chug, jerk, jerk, and then zoom away until we came to the next stop sign. Then the sequence would start again. The children actually scrunched down so no one could see them when we chugged along. They pleaded with me to drop them off a block from school so they wouldn't be embarrassed in front of their friends. I didn't relent to their desperate request even though I actually felt a little sorry for them as we traveled down that cartoony highway. But I had to take them to school; it was my job. A neighbor commented, "I can tell when you are taking the children to school because I hear you at the stop sign from inside my house."

I wasn't the only one driving down that standard-shift looney tune road; one afternoon my friend picked me up for a shopping trip to downtown Sharon. She stopped at a red light on State Street. We were on a steep incline and she rolled down her window, stuck her head out of the window, and yelled at the fellow in the car behind us, "You might want to back up a little; I'm driving a stick-shift car." This friend was a classmate who just a few years back had the audacity to laugh at my driving experiences in high school.

The standard-shift car wasn't the only one I drove down the looney tune boulevard. I found myself in a cartoony situation with every car we owned. One afternoon, I drove Marty to the mall, got out of the car, and locked the car doors. Suddenly I realized my keys were in the car. At first this didn't concern me since I locked my keys in the car many times before and all I had to do was call someone to bring me the spare set of keys. Then I would proceed on my way shopping until they got there. However, this time was a little different because I noticed a sound coming from the car. It was still running. I realized this situation needed to be settled quickly before I ran out of gas. Then I would be in a real predicament. I looked around the parking lot for help. I spotted a police car parked at the end of the lot watching traffic. Wow, was that luck. I sent Marty to tell the officer our problem. He came to my rescue with a tool and opened my car door.

One day Marty and I came out of the mall and got into my burgundy car. I put my key into the ignition and the key would not turn so I took the key out and put it carefully back into the ignition and it still would not turn. Then I noticed a can of cola in the cup tray that I do not drink and a jacket that was not mine. I looked out the window and noticed another burgundy car and suddenly realized that we were in the wrong car. We quickly jumped out of the car and dashed over to my car.

Twice in the bank parking lot I made macho men scream. The first time was when Tom drove me to the bank. I got out of the car and went into the bank and made my deposit. When I came out of the bank and got into the car I heard a loud scream. The loud scream scared me, so I screamed as I looked at the person behind the wheel. It wasn't Tom. Then I realized I got into the wrong car and scared the man behind the wheel. I immediately jumped out of the car and made sure Tom was behind the wheel before I got into another car.

The second time was when I drove to the bank. After I completed my transactions I went to the parking lot and opened the driver door of a red SUV. A strange man was sitting in the driver seat. He yelled because I scared him and I yelled because I was not expecting to see someone in the car. I apologized and went to my car. This wouldn't have been strange if I had driven the same type car he was sitting in; however, I forgot which car I drove and instead of getting into a big red SUV I walked over to my small blue car and got inside. I bet that fellow thought I was some weirdo.

Lora and I stopped at a local station for gas on our way to lunch. The first pump was out of order so I stopped at pump three and got out of the car, took off my gas cap, and went to get the nozzle. As I took off the nozzle, I noticed a girl coming out of the store. She caught my attention because she had a pink stripe in the center of her black hair. As she approached me, she revealed, "I prepaid $5.00 on that pump." So I handed her the nozzle. A car pulled up behind me so I pulled up to pump two so he could use pump four. I picked up the nozzle of pump two and headed for my car. The man who pulled up to pump four got out of his car and stated, "You have to prepay." I answered, "Oh." I put the nozzle back and went inside. The man at pump four got there before me and told the lady he wanted to prepay pump four for $20.00. She couldn't get the register to prepay pump four. She kept trying with no success. Finally she asked, "Did you take the nozzle off the pump?" He answered, "Yes, I put it into the gas tank." She revealed, "I can't set the pump to prepay with the nozzle off." He went to his car and put the nozzle back on the pump. Meanwhile, a fellow pulled up on the other side of pump two and proceeded to pump some gas into his truck while I was standing in line. Now inside the store it's my turn so I said, "I want to prepay $10.00 on pump two." However $20.00 kept showing up. I repeated, "I just wanted to prepay $10.00 not $20.00." So the clerk kept trying and it kept showing $20.00. Finally a fellow in line behind me apparently realized that pump two was the one he used to fill up his truck. So he stepped up and apologized, "I'm sorry I wasn't paying attention but pump two is the pump that I just used for my truck." So he went to the front of the line and paid the $20.00. I declared, "I thought you had to prepay." The clerk answered, "You can do it either way." I gave the clerk my $ 10.00 to prepay on pump two. By this time a line formed behind me. When I turned to leave, I noticed a lady staring at my hand. I always wear a plastic glove so I don't get gas on my hand when I pump gas. I forgot to take it off when I put the nozzle back. I guess this looked a little strange since I have never seen anyone pump gas with a plastic glove on. I don't understand why people don't wear a plastic glove when they pump gas.

I took my car to a garage to get it inspected. Later in the afternoon I called the garage to see if my car was ready. The receptionist called the service department and asked if my car was finished. After quite a while the receptionist told me, "They can't find your car. I will call you right back when they find it." I got off the phone and told Tom how stupid they were for losing my car.

Then Tom asked, "Who did you call?" I told him and he replied, "You called the wrong garage." I said, "Oops!" I immediately called the garage back and told them that I called them by mistake and that I had taken my car to another garage. I thought she would be annoyed but she sounded relieved. Then I called the right garage and picked up my car. These experiences with my car happened within a two-week period. I always say things like this happen to sharpen us up and it worked. Since then, I haven't left the keys in the car with it running, gotten into the wrong car, caused chaos at the gas pump, or called the wrong garage. However, something else happens and I sharpen up, then something else and something else. It never ends . . . .

YES! There were many experiences my friends witnessed over the years that led them to the conclusion that I was a "Cartoon Character" just like Tom. I guess I just didn't realize it since I was dealing with Tom's antics on a daily basis. These stories definitely indicate I am a *cartoon character* in every aspect of my existence as I journey along the trails of life.

3

I Am Surrounded
By Cartoon Characters

As I journeyed back in time I discovered many of my friends traveling down the looney tune trail beside me; therefore, I could not help being any other character while associating with them. The same people that were on my deck accusing me of being a cartoon character were a little hypocritical, because many times they were the cause or a major part of my cartoony experiences that led them to that conclusion. Also I observed the comical behavior of relatives, neighbors and strangers; I am surrounded by cartoon characters. It's no wonder I traveled down the looney trail so often. I am influenced and surrounded by their hilarious behavior, but I feel like I am the main character in comic land.

The next stories are about the friends that traveled down the looney tune exercise path with me. First, three friends I have known since seventh grade were always concerned about their weight. After having children we decided to firm up and lose a few pounds. We needed some incentive to exercise so we decided to have a contest. We all agreed to put $5.00 into a pot and whoever lost the most weight would win the money. Since we got together every other Friday to go shopping, this was a perfect time to weigh-in. I won the first weigh-in by only one pound. I knew I would really have to work hard for the next weigh-in since I was almost at my ideal weight. I would have to plan a really good strategy to win again. So on the day of the weigh-in, I took an enema to clean out all of the extra gunk from inside my body. It was well worth the extra effort because I won this time too! I beat the same person by a quarter of a pound. While I was collecting the money I made the mistake of saying, "Boy, am I glad I took that enema before I came here." The friend I beat by a quarter of a pound protested, "No fair, you are not allowed to take an enema!" I asked, "Why not?" No one else seemed to care either way. But she kept insisting that it wasn't fair. We took a vote. I won!

Next I purchased a membership at a local gym with a couple of friends that I met in scouting. We wanted to firm up and shed a few pounds and inches. We went to exercise classes and worked out on the equipment. Once a week we were weighed, measured, and disclosed what we ate that week. People would say, "I ate salad, fruit, vegetables, yogurt, and gelatin." When they were weighed and measured most of them gained weight and their body increased a couple of inches. When it was my turn, I was always reluctant to say what I ate because I was the only one that confessed, "I ate pizza, chilidogs, cheeseburgers, french fries, pie and ice cream." When I was weighed and measured I always lost a couple of pounds and inches. They were astonished and asked, "How did you lose weight eating like that?" I explained, "I ate half of a pizza instead of a whole pizza and I ate one cheeseburger instead of two." I finally tired of explaining myself to the salad eaters every week and being the target of their envy. They were either lying about what they ate or I have an excellent metabolism. Either way, I decided I had enough of paying someone to weigh me and tell me what to eat and how many sit ups to do. I already know what to do. All I had to do was to do it.

My next adventure to get into shape was joining a bowling league with my neighbor and a couple of friends. I only bowled Scotch Doubles with Tom and a few of our friends when we were first married, but I figured I knew enough about the game to join this league with my friends. I bought blue bowling shoes, a blue bowling ball, and a matching bag. The league started at 9:00 PM which was a perfect time. I wasn't even missed since Tom was on afternoon turn and I put the kids to bed before getting ready for bowling. I was so excited. I dressed in a light blue sweater and navy blue pants. I looked in the mirror and admired how cool I looked in my bowling outfit. When the sitter arrived, I went to the bowling alley. My friends, neighbor, and I were on the same team so we really enjoyed ourselves. I was bowling for a while when the owner came over and asked, "Do you play baseball?" Since I don't play baseball I thought that she had mistaken me for someone else, so I answered, "No." Then she rudely remarked, "Well the way you throw the ball down the alley when you bowl, you would probably be good at baseball." Away went all of my coolness with that one remark. After two years of bowling and no improvement or weight loss we decided to move on.

Next, a friend and I signed up for tennis lessons at a local club. I found an old racket in the attic and I bought a new shirt, matching shorts, and shoes. We were in a class with twenty ladies. In the first few lessons we learned how to hold the racket, serve, and the different swings. I mastered how to hold the racket, and it felt like I had pretty good form and a mean swing. I was really getting the hang of tennis. We were working on perfecting our backswing when I noticed the pro watching me. I thought, "Wow, he must be impressed with my swing. It is flawless. I can hit any ball. Come on; bring it on." Then I noticed him approaching me. I thought, "He must want me to demonstrate my perfect swing to the class." All eyes were always on him since he was a cool dude in his tennis outfit and everyone was competing for his attention. But he was approaching me. He asked to see my racket. Then I thought, "My racket must be valuable and caught his eye since it was in the attic forever." Then after looking it over he told me in front of the whole class, "No wonder you can't hit the ball properly, your tennis racket is warped." How could he make such a negative statement about how I hit the ball when I felt so good performing my flawless swings?

After our lessons ended, we tried to play a game of tennis. Since neither of us could get the ball over the net we decided to reserve the ball machine as our opponent. We set the machine to serve us the balls and took turns hitting them. We always hit the ball since the machine shot it in the exact same place every time, but where they landed was another story. We noticed we were annoying other players with our stray balls that bounced off the rafters, walls, ceiling, and onto their courts. We would eliminate part of the problem by reserving an end court. This way we only irritated one court. After many weeks of playing tennis with the ball machine, we never improved. We also sensed the nonverbal language from the attendant when we reserved the ball machine once again. We rationalized, "Why should they care how many times we reserve the machine since no one was using it and we were paying for the court." However, we finally decided to put away our crutch and play tennis with each other. This didn't work since after many tries one of us would finally serve the ball over the net and then the other couldn't hit it back. This was definitely harder than playing with the ball machine. We realized we would never be able to play tennis with a real person. We also noticed the nonverbal language from the pro and some others that often came to the courts. After much deliberation, we relented to sitting in the lounge by the window that overlooked the tennis courts and watched others play the game of tennis while sipping on wine and snacking.

Around this time I gave up on exercise since I was busy caring for my three children. Again, I found myself wandering down the cartoony trail with my friends as we went about our daily routine. One afternoon, my neighbor visited with her three children. The visit only lasted fifteen minutes since her three children and my three children were constantly getting into mischief. Their ages were one, two, four, five, seven and eight. After fifteen minutes, she gathered her children and said, "I'll come back in ten years."

A week later I called her and suggested we try a day at the lake with our six children. We packed a picnic lunch, sand buckets, and loaded the children into the van. They played in the sand and water without quarreling. The afternoon was very enjoyable until some young girls flaunted their shapely, slim, tanned bodies around in their teeny, weenie bikinis in front of us. They reminded us of a time not too long ago at this same lake when we were the young girls, flaunting our young, slim, tan, vibrant bodies. We pranced along the shore in our one piece bathing suits with the wind blowing through our hair. We envisioned ourselves as we once were at this lake and for a brief time we were teenagers again without a care in the world. Our focus was on the cool life guard and the other hunks riding the waves. That was a time before the arrival of the six children running wildly around us. Now my friend and I felt a little imperfect as we looked down at our aging, unshapely, pale bodies. Our bodies were defective and had definite signs of wear complete with stretch marks and varicose veins. This was the direct result of being pregnant for twenty-seven months, delivering three children, caring for them and doing housework. We felt like beached whales as beneath us the gritty sand slid and shifted under the weight of our bodies. The fine grains of sand were sticking to the sweat on our legs, arms, and neck as we sat under the hot noon sun caring for our children.

After a while of watching these young girls, we came up with a game. I fantasized that whenever I looked at a bikini babe and said the word, "ZAP" then the bikini babe and I would instantly exchange bodies. We "ZAPPED" all afternoon laughing hysterically of how surprised the bikini babes would be if their tan, slim, flawless bodies suddenly changed into our nearly thirty bulging, pale bodies. While we were "Zapping", a vision flashed through my mind and I told my friend, "It would just be my luck to "Zap" one who had an incurable disease and was about to die in a few weeks." She replied, "It would be my luck to "Zap" one who was *pregnant!*" We laughed hysterically at that thought. We had so much fun with the children at the lake that summer, we decided to spend the next few summers wading, sunbathing, and "Zapping" at the lake.

Another friend and I strolled down the looney tune navigation trail when we decided to take our children to Sea World. I told her I would be the driver if she would be the navigator since I always got lost. I arrived at her house early in the morning and we started off on our new adventure.

I got us as far as route 305; now it was her turn to get us the rest of the way and back home. After a while she replied, "Turn right at the little white church." I drove on then she instructed, "Turn at the big maple tree." Later she informed, "Turn at the house with the pretty bay window." Fifteen minutes later we finally arrived at Sea World.

Everyone had a wonderful time watching the exciting shows and munching on the delicious food. We all headed to the parking lot expressing our favorite parts of the shows. The exhausted children settled themselves into the back of the van, and I headed out of the parking lot toward the road. I knew we were in trouble when she replied, "Turn right." I positively knew we turned left because I always fret when I have to make a left turn. I was absolutely sure that on the way out I would have to make a left turn because I was concerned about it all day. She insisted, "Turn right! Right!" Suddenly my mind flashed back to my first driving lesson when I was headed toward a field and my driving teacher shouted, "Turn left! Left!" In spite of her insistence I turned left out of the parking lot and before long she realized I was right; however, she didn't have a clue as to how to get home. Now in the dark and going in the opposite direction, I wondered how we were going to find the little white church, the big maple tree, the house with the pretty bay window. Even if we found them we didn't know which way to turn. Here we were lost before we made the first turn out of the parking lot with five exhausted children squirming in the back. We looked at each other and laughed hysterically. When I regained my composure, I drove around trying to find something that looked familiar. After a few stops to ask for directions, we were finally on familiar territory and made our way home past the little white church, the big maple tree, and the house with the pretty bay window. This was a perfect example of driving down the looney tune trail with my friend navigating.

The next time I picked her up for a trip she jumped into my van with the biggest ledger I had ever seen. She proudly announced, "This time we won't get lost on the way home. I will write down the route numbers, names of the streets, and which direction to turn." We didn't get lost.

A few years later two of my friends and I felt our minds needed a little exercise so we strolled down the education trail and enrolled in classes at a trade school. We took shorthand and a few other classes. We would go to lunch and study afterward. One day at lunch one friend opened her book and almost every word was highlighted in florescent pink. My friend and I both looked at her book at the same time and burst into laughter. Finally my friend asked, "Why did you highlight so much?" Clueless she answered, "I only highlighted the most important things." My friend suggested, "It would have been better if you highlighted what wasn't important."

It seemed no matter what I did with my friends eventually we ended up on that inevitable trail of cartoons. Three friends I knew since junior high and I formed a card club. The plan was once a month to have dinner at a restaurant and play cards afterward. After dinner we went to a room downstairs to play. There were a few tables of serious card-playing women. We could tell they were serious by the tension in the air. We went to a table and got out our cards and discovered that we had forgotten how to play the game. However, after putting our four heads together it didn't take long to remember enough to get us started, or at least we thought. The dealer shuffled the cards and asked, "How many cards do we get?" After more pondering, we couldn't come up with a number. The brave one of our bunch asked some of the other ladies who were playing cards if they knew how many cards to deal; they knew and we were on our way. This might be a clue of where our card club was going.

One of my friends liked to play bingo, and she talked me and a couple other friends into going with her. We were looking forward to a relaxing evening of small talk. Much to our surprise, our friend played twenty-five bingo cards and she didn't allow us to talk. We didn't realize she took her bingo playing so seriously. We sat for four hours playing our three bingo cards bursting at the seams to speak.

Three of my friends and I decided to go shopping for the day at a mall twenty miles away. My friend picked me up at the crack of dawn, and we decided to start off the day with breakfast. There was only one other person in the restaurant since it was so early. After breakfast we got into her car and my friend put the car into reverse and zoomed backward and crashed into the only car in the parking lot. A man came running out of the restaurant yelling, "Oh no, you smashed my new car! What's wrong with you? Can't you see?" It's hard to watch a grown man cry over his new toy. Apparently he just bought the car the day before. Needless to say, our shopping trip was ruined, especially since my friend had to go to her insurance company and report the accident. It wouldn't have been so bad if she hadn't worked for the same insurance company and had reported off work sick that morning so she could go shopping.

Another time my friend decided to take the day off work and go shopping. While we were looking at clothes, I notice her bend down behind the clothes racks. She kept moving around like she was hiding from someone. I bent down and asked her, "What's wrong?"

She whispered, "Shhh, that's my boss's wife over there." Apparently she reported off work sick again.

One of my classmates' mother died and I went to the funeral home with a couple of my friends to pay our respects. One friend gets so nervous at funeral homes, so she wanted to go first. I overheard her say to the family, "Congratulations." She was so nervous that she didn't even realize she said congratulations until we told her later.

After all my children were in school, I looked forward to meeting my friends for breakfast or lunch. Once we stayed so long and got so involved in our conversation that we were still carrying on our discussion as we walked out of the restaurant. We continued to chat in the parking lot when we noticed a waiter coming out of the restaurant and running toward us shouting, "You didn't pay your bills!" We were so embarrassed we said, "We aren't going back inside the restaurant." We each handed him ten dollars that would more than pay our bill and said, "Keep the change."

The subject of doctors came up when I was at breakfast with some of my friends. One friend confessed, "My doctor is constantly asking me if I have any problems. I always tell him everything is fine even though my feet are constantly hurting. At my last appointment I finally told him, 'My feet ache all the time.' He looked at me and replied, "Well look at those little feet and all the weight they have to carry around all day. You would hurt too if you had to carry that much weight around all day." She declared, "I will never complain to the doctor again." This led to long discussions of doctors, ailments, and pregnancy. Another friend stated after we each relived our painful labors in the delivery room, "I don't remember any labor pains or anything that went on in the delivery room because I went blind and was more stressed out about not being able to see." Apparently, she lost her sight temporarily from a panic attack; I never heard of it before or since but she actually went blind for a day. We stayed at breakfast so long that it was time for lunch so we simply went to another restaurant for lunch and continued our discussion.

Another friend I met for lunch came running into the restaurant and over to my table and shouted, "You will never guess what just happened! I can't go back to work after lunch!" I asked,

"What happened?" She replied, "I am so embarrassed!" Again I asked, "What happened?" She answered, "Well, my boss was talking to a salesman and when I went past them on my way out to lunch, I overheard my boss say to the salesman, 'Yes, sometimes you have to rob Peter to pay Paul.' Then I said to my boss, "Yes, sometimes don't you wish you had two Peters?" They looked at each other and roared laughing as they turned to look at me. I then realized my comment came across different than what I had intended. So I turned and ran out the door. Now how do I go back after that exit?" I replied, "Well, hope the salesman is gone when you go back."

Recently I called a friend and asked, "The church bulletin had an invitation for parish women to attend a luncheon. Would you like to go with me?" She answered, "Oh, I think just old ladies go to that lunch." Laughingly, I said to my friend, "What do you think we are?" She hesitated a minute then laughingly said, "Well, I'm seventy two." I laughed and said, "Yeah and I'm sixty-nine." We went to lunch and fit right in with the old ladies. One lady moved her cane so we could sit down and said, "We are just talking about therapy." I said, "Really I just got out of therapy for my hip."

Another lady said, "I almost didn't come today. I checked my answering machine earlier and a friend called and left a message saying, "Do you want a ride to lunch tomorrow?" I thought lunch was changed till tomorrow until she called a little while ago and asked, "Are you going to lunch today?" Apparently she called Tuesday and I didn't check my machine until Wednesday and thought lunch was changed to Thursday.

They told funny stories and were a joy to be with. One lady said, "My son is getting an award and has to speak at the awards banquet. He recently fell and knocked a tooth out and his temporary tooth slides out when he talks. Then he just fell again and broke his arm. He took his suit to get the one sleeve removed so he could fit his arm through. When he went to pick up his jacket they had removed the wrong sleeve. However, he discovered the cast would slip through the sleeve, so they sewed it back on." I can't wait until next month to see how his speech went.

One afternoon a friend and I were upstairs in the spare room working on a project for a religious class we were teaching at church. After a while we started discussing the priest. At that very instant we heard a loud noise and the house shook. We instantly stopped talking and looked at each other thinking this must be a divine intervention for us to stop gossiping. After we regained our senses, we hurried downstairs and went outside to investigate what caused the incident. All the neighbors were outside wondering what had happened. We didn't disclose we thought we were the cause since we were gossiping about the priest. Later, we discovered there was a slight earthquake in the area. We felt guilty discussing the priest and wonder to this day if this was a sign from God for us to stop *gossiping*.

One summer, Tom and his buddy went to the "Indianapolis 500" for the weekend. His wife and their two children stayed with me and my two children while they were gone. We spent the day entertaining the children at the park. After we put the children to bed, we planned to relax by devouring appetizers and our favorite drink 7&7, so we went to the liquor store to get the 7&7. I parked in front and started into the store while my friend stayed in the car with the four children. I didn't get too far when I realized I didn't know what the bottle of liquor was called. (This was when you went to the counter and told the attendant what liquor you wanted and he went into the back room for your order.) So I went back to the car and we pondered about how to order the liquor. We knew it was a fraction, but couldn't remember if it was a third, a half, or a fourth. Finally I remembered it was a fifth. So I proceeded into the liquor store and said, "I would like a fifth of 7&7. The fellow behind the counter began to laugh and informed me, "I can give you the fifth of liquor but you will have to go down the street to the grocery store and get the 7-up." I guess I ordered a drink.

Tom and his friends were waiting to board a plane for a golf trip. One of the fellows was deathly afraid of flying so he had a few drinks while waiting. He was drinking whiskey from mini-bottles that came in a nice purple sack with gold letters. It was just the right size for golf tees. The good thing was he drank so much that, all twelve guys got a purple sack. The bad thing was he almost wasn't allowed on the plane. Tom still carries his purple bag in his golf bag.

One of my friends is always zapping me with some of her words of wisdom. While I was visiting her I was complaining about all the damage my three children do to the walls and woodwork. She pointed out the nicks on her walls and furniture from her children. She caringly replied, "These will be sweet reminders of the children when they move." I felt a little guilty complaining about my nicks. I never thought of the nicks in that way before; hence, at this moment I saw my nicks in a new light. I now had many memorial nicks throughout my house. I was shocked when shortly after her children moved out she sold her house for a nice new no-nick one and here I sit in my nicked house of memories.

The next few stories are observations of people going down that cartoon trail at the local tavern. One New Year's Eve party, at midnight an elderly gentleman started kissing all the women. He started at one end of the room, and when he was halfway through the tavern I noticed him approaching a fellow with long curly hair (a time when men didn't wear their hair long). I nudged Tom and asked, "Is he going to kiss him?" I no sooner got those words out of my mouth when he reached over and kissed the fellow. When he realized he had kissed a fellow, his New Year's Eve quest ended.

A fellow came into a local tavern and said to the fellow sitting next to us, "I'm not here; I just came to tell you I wasn't coming."

A bookstore chain was going bankrupt and closing all their stores. Every day the books were discounted more and more. A fellow sitting next to us at the bar said, "I received an e-mail from the book store in Niles saying they have 90% off all the books in the store. I called and they didn't answer their phone. I thought they were really busy so I jumped into my car and drove twenty miles to the bookstore. Would you believe it was closed?"

A lady stood beside us and called the bartender over and handed him three dollars. She confessed, "Last night someone dared me to drink that shot you put on the bar. When no one was looking I walked up to the bar and drank it. Whose shot was that anyway and what was it?" The bartender didn't remember putting the shot on the bar. However, she insisted he take the three dollars.

Cartoon characters are everywhere. There isn't a day that goes by that I don't run into one traveling down that cartoony trail. I attended a dinner with Tom at one of his organizations. I noticed the foot from panty hose sticking out of the bottom of the pants of one woman sitting at the head table. She pranced around from table to table, working the room, talking to everyone. Well into the evening, I noticed her walk into the rest room. When she came out, the foot of the panty hose was gone. She apparently discovered her wardrobe miss function. Evidently, she took off her pantyhose and slacks together and when she put on her slacks again, she didn't notice the pantyhose were still in her slacks. I have done this a few times myself; fortunately, I discovered it before I left the house.

I was going down an aisle at the grocery store and a lady backed into my buggy as I walked passed her. She said, "I'm sorry, I'm just floating around here." A little later I noticed a stock boy with a load of boxes patiently waiting at the end of an aisle for someone to move from the middle of the aisle. I looked down the aisle and there was the same lady that had backed into me standing in the middle of the isle staring at the merchandise. After shopping, I went to the parking lot and noticed the same lady wandering around. She walked past my car and looked at me and said, "We meet again." I asked, "Did you lose your car?" She answered, "Yes, I should know better than to go shopping on my lunch hour."

Just when I think I am a little nutty someone tops my craziness. I was coming out of the grocery store and approaching my car at the same time another lady was going to her car. There was an empty parking space between us. When she got to her car I noticed her rubbing her front fender that had a large white scratch and a small dent. Then I heard her say, "Those B@@@@##S! Some B@@@@###D hit my car! Look what that B@@@@##d did to my car! Now what in the H#@L am I going to do! Those B@@@@##S!" I said, "Gee, they had plenty of room. These parking spaces are actually big." She went around to the driver's side still cussing while she opened the door and got in. While I was putting my groceries into the trunk, I noticed her get out of the car and walk around to the front of the car. My first thought was, "She must be going to call the police." Then I heard her say, "This isn't my car! The doors opened with my key! Why did they open with my key? This isn't my car!" We both started laughing and she looked relieved as she walked past me to her car on the other side of the parking lot.

These are the stories that prove there are tons of cartoon characters out there. People not only act like cartoon characters they also dress like one. Many of them can be found at the coffee shop we go to regularly. One afternoon, I noticed a young fellow sitting alone in a booth. He had upon his head the craziest looking hat. It was a cross between the Orville brothers' pilot hat and Santa's elves hats. He got the attention of everyone who walked by. I couldn't imagine why a young man would wear this hat. Then I noticed the young girls' reaction as they walked past him. They couldn't resist stroking his hat and making comments. He just smiled. His cartoony hat was a chick magnet.

Then a mother and daughter strolled by wearing large, bulky, quilted, matching vests. They looked like two lost hunters straight out of the forest scurrying around.

The next time one of my friends accuse me of being a cartoon character I will reply, "It takes one to know one and you are the biggest one." These stories certainty prove beyond a shadow of a doubt that I am not the only one traveling down the looney tune trail, and many times someone is traveling right along with me.

4

Tom Will Always
Be a Cartoon Character

While I was journeying back in time it became clearer that Tom was a cartoon character with his bizarre Lally Logic as early as when we first met and I just hadn't noticed. I guess at age twelve I was blinded by youth, inexperience, or was just naive. Why did I think his behavior in typing and music class was so cute? How could I think his loud obnoxious burp at "The Burp" was so adorable? His lack of observation at the drive-in when he drove off from the parking place with the speaker still in the window as well as the cord blowing in the wind was surely a hint. Especially the way we made our getaway somewhat like Bonnie and Clyde. Maybe these behaviors were an indicator that I was in the presence of a cartoon character and was so blinded by his charm that I didn't notice. I recalled only that it was funnier then. Everything was funnier.

I interpret events a little different now than when I was a teenager, since I see a side of him nowadays that I didn't see then. Our honeymoon sure was an indicator. We married in 1964 and I observed some of Tom's strange thinking when he failed to make reservations for our honeymoon, and we couldn't find a room on our wedding night. When I asked, "Why didn't you make reservations for our honeymoon?" His logic was, "This is Erie not New York. You don't have to make a reservation here." I thought, "Why not? Motels get full in any town, and wouldn't he want to make sure he got a room on such a special night." This was some bizarre thinking. As a result we had to spend our wedding night in a rundown hotel with prostitutes roaming in front of the hotel and lobby. (For more detail refer to chapter one of *Help! I Married a Cartoon Character.*)

Another tip was a few months after we were married when I flew to North Carolina where he was stationed in the Air Force. The time I spent with him in North Carolina was great. He showed me around the town and took me shopping at the PX. We spent an afternoon at one of his friend's home, and his wife fixed a delicious Southern meal. He got a weekend pass to drive me home. We stopped at a grocery store and Tom sent me in to get a pound of garlic bologna and a package of buns. At the time I didn't realize he planned a marathon trip of five hundred miles, only stopping for gas. It wouldn't have been so bad, but I was one month pregnant and felt a little nauseous. Garlic bologna wasn't something my stomach could tolerate, and the smell of garlic on his breath for five hundred miles added to the nausea. I asked him to stop at a restaurant a couple of times but he said, "I'm not hungry." Needless to say I was woozy, starving, thirsty, and wasn't speaking to him for most of the trip. Finally he stopped at a restaurant two miles from home. I still didn't have too much to say to him. He asked, "Why are you so annoyed? You got to eat, didn't you?" His logic, "If I feed her before we get home she won't have any reason to be angry." This sure was a red flag.

At some point I realized I married a cartoon character and in 2007 I wrote a book about his cartoon adventures and peculiar logic. You would think someday the cartoony experiences would stop, but they didn't. They just keep happening and happening. Tom journeys through life along the cartoon trail and there is no end to his encounters.

Shortly after Tom returned from the service we started looking for a place to rent because I lived at home while he was in the Air Force and we weren't ready to buy a house yet. We checked many rental properties, and Tom was never satisfied. Finally, he came across an apartment complex under construction in Sharpsville. A section with four apartments was just completed and ready for renters. He wanted to move into one. I told him I was leery of the apartments since they were connected. I always lived in the country and had a great deal of land to roam around. I didn't want to share a backyard with strangers. I had visions of me in my living room sneezing and someone in the next apartment saying, "Bless you." However he assured me that these new apartments were sound proof and if we rented an end apartment we would only be near one other renter. He pointed out the large pool, spacious backyards, and each apartment had a patio. His "logic" sounded reasonable so I agreed to move into the apartment. Of course, the end apartments were taken by the time we got an appointment with the realtor, so I was in an apartment with renters attached on both sides.

It didn't take me to long to discover the new apartment wasn't sound proof. Since our bathrooms were back-to-back, I could clearly hear the other tenants running their water and talking in their bathroom. I am sure they could hear me, too. This is why I didn't want to live here! Sound proof, my foot!

One hot summer afternoon I put Maureen down for her nap. Then I changed into my bathing suit and headed for my patio to soak up some rays. When I opened my patio doors, low and behold, there was a man sunning with his bulges showing in his skimpy Speedo, sucking up my rays. Our patios were connected and a thin crack in the cement separated them. I shut the door and sucked in the rays of the light bulb and cursed Tom. This is why I didn't want to live here! As for the spacious backyard, our complex was at the bottom of a hill and I had five feet of yard to roam around. I was surrounded by apartment complexes, and I always felt like someone was watching me.

A few days later a salesman came to the door selling the perfect five-in-one piece of baby furniture. He explained, "This one piece of furniture will accommodate every need of your baby. It is a high chair, car seat, swing, baby seat, walker, and stroller all in one. It will save you space and money." Thank goodness I had experience with my baby brothers and sister and knew what a hassle it would be to assemble and disassemble that one piece of furniture to meet the baby's needs throughout the day. So I sent him on his way.

Later that evening, we went to visit friends. Tom told them about the salesman and the contraption he was selling. Tom then proceeded to say, "That five-in-one devise is really impractical and anyone who bought the contraption had to be an idiot." He explained, "Every time you went somewhere you had to take apart the highchair and construct a car seat, then take the car seat apart and put together a stroller, then take apart the stroller and assemble the car seat, then take the car seat back into the house and create a highchair or walker or swing. Then when you went somewhere you started the whole cycle all over again. I don't know of anyone who would buy that contraption, but I guess there is a sucker born every day." Our friend left the room and came in carrying the device and announced, "Hello! Meet the sucker of the day!"

One night we opened the windows to let in the cool fresh air and the neighbors were having a party that went on well into the night. Tom couldn't sleep, but he wasn't going to complain and admit it was a huge mistake moving here. Finally, at 2:00 AM the last of their company was leaving and the fellow in the adjoining apartment shouted, "Come back again." The fellow getting into his car replied, "Is tomorrow too soon?" That comment struck our funny bone or we were just exhausted because Tom and I laughed hysterically. I am sure the neighbors heard us and wondered what in the world we were doing. For the next few months whenever we went anywhere and someone said, "Come back again," Tom just couldn't resist replying, "Is tomorrow too soon?"

We lived in the apartment for a year, and then we bought a house. I was adamant about having plenty of room between me and my neighbors. I made sure I didn't listen to any more of his sound proof logic. We found a house in the north side of Sharpsville, and I couldn't be happier. We walked through the living room and into the hall and looked down into our sunken kitchen. We were in awe of how beautiful it looked. Our house was on two lots and next to the last house on a dead-end street. Our backyard and side yards meet the back and side yards of our neighbors. I can talk, sit on my patio, and sleep without hearing the neighbors.

However, I hate to admit it, but there was a tiny downfall of living here. I see more critters here than I did living out in the country. Our yard is a playground for deer, ground hogs, squirrels, and rabbits. But the varmints we feared and tried to avoid were the skunks. However, we had two encounters with them. This time, a skunk didn't fall through the cellar window (The first skunk story is in chapter five of "*Help! I Married a Cartoon Character*"). It was on our patio when we came home late one night. After the last episode of the skunk in the house, I begged Tom to do something about the skunks roaming around our yard at night. He gave me some of his nature logic and there we were face to face with another skunk. We spotted it and slowly backed off. We went to the front door but couldn't get in since the storm door was locked from the inside. We knocked on the door, but the children didn't wake up so we went to a tavern to call. (Before cell phones) They didn't answer the phone. We drove home and patiently waited in the car for the skunk to leave. An hour later, the skunk finally left. Then we quickly bolted into the house. Skunks in cartoons may be friendly, but these were not!

The cartoony experiences never stop. Tom just continues down that looney tune trail. One summer morning, I was sitting in the kitchen sipping on my tea when I heard a commotion coming from the garage. By the time I got to the patio, Tom was staggering in. I ran over to see if he was all right and asked, "What happened?" He said, "I was lighting the pilot light on the hot water tank and the torch leaked and burst into flames. I ran out of the garage with the flaming propane torch and tripped head over heels into the driveway while throwing the torch into the yard." I asked, "Why were you lighting the hot water tank with a torch?" He answered, "I always light it with a torch." I thought, "Don't most people light a water tank with a match or a lighter?" He completely ignores the fact that he started the fire and considers himself a hero for saving the garage from burning down.

Tom has always prided himself on being aware of his surroundings; however, his observations over the years have proved the exact opposite. He not only can't see what's right in front of him, but he also doesn't listen. He often accuses me of hiding things in plain sight. Tom will always eat the whole bag of treats, and when I go for a snack, all I find is an empty bag. So I put the treats in the center of the lower cupboards, and since he won't bend, they are safe. The treats last for weeks. He always says, "You hide things in plain sight." Yes, I do hide things in plain sight. All he has to do is bend.

The ultimate was when we went to the water slides with some of our friends. We sat in an area at the bottom of the slides so we could watch our children slide down into the water and cheer them on. Some adults went on the slides, and for some reason unknown to me water always attracts the savage, tanned, well-endowed, bikini babes. No sense talking to the guys when they came sliding down the slide for all their attention was on the babes. Suddenly, I noticed one of the babes splashing out of control as she slid down the slide and—*splat!*—Into the water she flew. Well her cute little bikini top slid down to her waist from the impact of the water. She got out of the water a little dazed and pranced right past us. I felt a cool breeze as she passed from her boobs flopping back and forth in every direction. We were speechless and watched her in disbelief. Her friends were frantically trying to get her attention, but she kept walking in the opposite direction. Finally, she realized her wardrobe malfunction and screamed from embarrassment, which only drew more attention to her. She immediately pulled her bikini top up and ran off. All this happened over a course of a few minutes. When we composed ourselves, the fellows started to crack jokes and Tom was clueless. He was sitting among us and missed all the excitement. Yes, the fellow who prides himself of being aware of his surroundings was yet again *unaware*.

One night, Tom was playing a Star Trek Game on his computer that he had received on his 40th birthday. He has been a great fan of the Star Trek show for many years and has seen every episode many times. At midnight, I asked Tom when he was coming to bed. He was so wrapped up in the game, he answered, "I'll beam up in a minute!" He was totally serious when he said this.

Tom was cleaning the trash container and asked, "Where is the Lysol?" I answered, "It's on the kitchen counter." A little later, I went to put the cleaners away and I noticed the furniture polish can was all sticky. I asked Tom, "Were you using the furniture polish for anything? It's all sticky." He answered, "No, I just used the Lysol spray." I said, "I don't have Lysol spray, just the liquid in the bottle." He cleaned the trash container with furniture polish and didn't know the difference!

Tom had just bought the latest high-tech camera and was excited about trying it out on the pro golfers at the practice rounds at the Masters. He positioned himself so he could get exceptional pictures of the golfer's technique and the beautiful landscape in the background. He intently watched all the pro golfers and patiently waited for the perfect shot. He was constantly bragging, "Boy, that was a great shot. Wow, did you see that impressive shot I just took? Look at the fantastic view in the background." About half way around the course, he asked me to walk across a bridge so he could take my picture with the scenic view in the background. Shortly after this picture, he discovered he hadn't inserted the film into the camera properly. (Before digital cameras) The Masters practice was half over, and Tom didn't have any pictures. I went back to the first hole with the low-tech cameraman with his high-tech camera and started all over again. Take two!

Tom was taking the air conditioner out of the window in the spare room and I told him, "When you put the air conditioner into the attic make sure you push it over to the side. Keep the middle clear so I can get to the decorations and other things stored in the attic." He ignored me. I repeated, "Push the air conditioner to the side." He didn't answer. Again I said, "Tom! Make sure you push the air conditioner to the side." Finally, he replied, "I will take care of it. Why don't you go downstairs? I can handle this." So I reluctantly went downstairs.

When I went into the attic in the fall for the decorations I could not believe my eyes. There in the center of the attic was the air conditioner. I couldn't get to the back of the attic without bumping into the containers. I thought, "Why couldn't he just slide the air conditioner to the side like I asked? I won't ask him why. I don't want to hear any of his air logic excuses."

Tom was walking down the sidewalk from his mother's house to our car. He heard a neighbor yell from across the street, "Hi, how are you doing?" Tom looked up and shouted, "Hi, okay." Then Tom heard the voice of another neighbor behind him and realized the neighbor wasn't talking to him but to the neighbor down the street. Neither of them noticed or heard Tom, but I did. This was very humorous to witness and I won't let him forget it. Oh, my cartoon character!

A friend of my granddaughter was visiting and a neighbor was riding a three wheeler in their backyard. Hattie's friend shouted, "There's my friend riding a three wheeler." Tom asked, "How do you know it's your friend? It might be her older brother." I answered, "Tom, pink jacket, pink helmet with long blond hair blowing in the wind. I'm sure her brother wouldn't be wearing pink, and besides he doesn't have long blond hair.

Tom's singing is looney, not *Tunney*. He calls it Lally Tunes. Every once in a while a favorite song of Tom's is sung at church, and he will start to sing a few words. When I notice people looking our way, I nudge him or give him the *look* and he immediately stops. I am afraid if he continues to sing, the stain glass will break out of the windows or the church will come tumbling down. Sometimes the church choir announces they need people to sing in the choir. Tom says, "I think I will join and see if they kick me out." I say, "Remember eighth grade music, do, re, me."

A local organization has an annual celebration every March and a band from Toronto arrives every year to march in the parade. After the parade, refreshments are served at the club and some of the fellows entertain us with their music and singing. Tom and I were talking to some of the singers and Tom told them, "I really enjoyed your singing even though I can't sing a note." They stated, "Anyone can sing." So a group of them worked with Tom trying to get him to carry a tune. They sang one note and asked him to repeat it. Tom would repeat the notes; however, they didn't sound the same. They tried note after note, and Tom never hit one. Eventually, one by one the singers left and only one determined singer remained with Tom. After half an hour, he finally gave up. This proves Tom's singing is definitely the Looney Tunes.

He's also a little looney when it comes to interior design, and I'm not the only one who thinks so. Tom comes up with the weirdest combinations of colors and designs when we want to remodel. He frustrates me with his suggestions. He also irritated an interior decorator when we were picking out fabric for our sofa. He kept bringing over fabric that didn't match, and finally the interior decorator lost patience and asked in a slightly raised irritated voice, "Will you please put that back!"

We recently remodeled the kitchen. After I stripped all the wallpaper off of the walls, I asked Tom to go with me and pick out the paint. He suggested that we hire someone to paint. I told him, "The hard work was done and I always painted the rooms over the years." However, he insisted with his no painting logic, "We are too old to be climbing up and down ladders." So he called a friend who painted in his spare time. His logic was ludicrous, since the friend he called was retired and as old as we are. He graduated from the next town and celebrated his 50ᵗʰ class reunion a week after our celebration.

Tom is the biggest baby and has a low tolerance for pain. Once he was lying on the sofa and suddenly started groaning in pain. I asked, "What's wrong, Tom?" He bellowed "Something is stabbing me. There is a needle or knife on the couch stabbing me!" I replied, "There can't be a needle or knife on the couch." He continued moaning, so I went over and looked where he was pointing and I saw a toothpick stuck on his shirt. I revealed, "Tom, it's a toothpick, not a needle or knife." Oh, my brave cartoon character!

Tom just has to hear of someone being sick and before long he complains of the same symptoms. When any of our children were sick, I tried to keep it from him as long as I could because before long he would moan and I would have two sick patients on my hands. One real and the other imagined. His most sickly looney statements were, "I'm almost sick. I'm half sick."

Many times Tom even looks cartoony. One afternoon he left the house with his grandson to run some errands. He went to the bank, post office, and shopping at a couple stores. I didn't pay much attention to him when he left because I was babysitting; however, when he came home and walked into the patio, I noticed he had his shirt on inside out and backwards. There was a tag just beneath his chin and large seams along his arms, neck, and waist. On the back was a large blurry decal. I said, laughing, "You have your shirt on inside out and backwards." He answered, "I wondered why everyone was staring at my shirt. I just thought they must think I am cool." One little girl I was babysitting couldn't stop laughing when he walked into the patio. When he made the statement that he was cool she laughed hysterically. I asked my grandson, "Didn't you notice Pa Pa's shirt?" He answered, "No."

I sold more than five hundred copies of the book I wrote about Tom: "*Help! I Married a Cartoon Character.*" All of these were bought by relatives and friends. However, they must have shared the book with their friends because strangers will approach Tom and ask, "So how is the Cartoon Character?" The last time Tom went for a blood test the lady taking his information asked, "Are you by any chance the "Cartoon Character." He was surprised and answered, "Yes."

When we were in Texas visiting my daughter, the school where she teaches was having a book fair. Tom and I were part of the program. The students were given a list of things they had to find in the book store, such as a mystery book, cookbook, Mother Goose, cartoon character, and an autograph from an author. Tom was the cartoon character in the coffee shop and I was the author doing a book signing. Tom cherishes the reality that he is referred to as a cartoon character that lives by logic of his own making.

5

The Cartoon Characters Reproduce

For sure, Tom and I have definitely journeyed down the looney tune trail many times and proved beyond a shadow of a doubt that we are definitely cartoon characters. One might wonder why in the world we would bring three more cartoon characters into the world. However, at the time we were planning a family, we weren't aware of traveling the looney trail and I was still trying to figure out Tom's logic.

Our first child, Maureen, was a perfect example of a model child so every step of her development went smoothly. She crawled, sat up, walked, talked, and I gave up her bottle right on schedule. When she was eighteen months old, I bought her a potty chair and training pants. I told her, 'You are a big girl now." Within a week she was potty trained. It was that easy. She was happy, outgoing, and very cooperative. No signs of traveling down the looney parenting trail.

Since we were naturals at childrearing we were excited when our second child, Lora, arrived. However, it didn't take us long to realize that we were not naturals at childrearing. She fought us every step in her development. Before she could crawl she would shimmy across the floor and get into trouble. She walked at ten months and threw the cushions off the sofa and tossed everything within her reach. She talked but wouldn't listen to a thing we said. She rebelled when we stopped giving her a bottle by taking tantrums at bedtime. She cared less about the potty and would pick it up and throw it. She was stubborn and uncooperative.

At this time, our parenting looney world began and Tom started wandering along the trail when he was alone with the toddler. One afternoon when I came home, the kitchen cupboards were trashed and flour was scattered all over. I confronted him about the mess and his nurturing logic surfaced, "She was quiet so I thought she wasn't getting into trouble."

A couple of weeks later, she asked him something and even though he didn't understand a word she spoke, he answered, "Okay." A few minutes later the neighbor called and informed us, "Your toddler is walking down the street toward the playground. My husband is following her to make sure she is all right while I called you." Apparently she asked him if she could go to the playground and he answered, "Okay." He hadn't a clue what she said.

Then along came Marty. We thought it couldn't be any more stressful than it already was. We were wrong. Now we had two in diapers. It was perplexing that every time I walked through the door when Tom was looking after the little ones a horrible smell was always coming from one of their diapers. When I questioned him, "Why didn't you change the diaper?" He would always reply with some innocent stinky logic, "They just did it right before you walked through the door." I could buy this a few times, but every time? No way.

When they were a little older, I discovered Tom was falling asleep instead of tending to the children, and they would watch scary programs on the television. One evening Maureen was in bed and called downstairs for me to come up and take a toy horse out of her bedroom. I asked her why she wanted the horse out of her room. She answered, "That horse is looking at me. It looks just like the one in the scary movie that I watched last night." Apparently, when her daddy was looking after her, he fell asleep and she viewed a scary movie that she was not allowed to watch. Of course, Marty had to sneak the toy horse back into her room every night just to torment her.

Tom added to their terror by telling them a spooky story he make up about the walking leg. Of course, the walking leg was in the yard so they were afraid to go outside. This was the start of the children waking up in the middle of the night with nightmares.

Tom is pathetic when he is losing a game. However, I thought he would change his attitude when playing with his young children. He didn't! I tried to persuade him to just play for fun and he quoted me some of his pathetic competitive logic. "There is no sense to play if not to win," he said. I fail to see the satisfaction in winning when he has an unfair advantage against little children who are just learning to play the games. When he plays scrabble, if he is losing, he will scatter the pieces all over the board. In monopoly, he gets annoyed when someone will not sell him their property so he can put up a hotel and bankrupt anyone landing on his place. He thinks his strategy is the only strategy. If he is losing he will eventually flip the board. However, if he is winning it's a different story. Everyone has to revel in his victory to the bitter end.

The journey down the parenting trail was difficult for the first few years because children come into the world so helpless and are dependent for so long. They were a clean slate and teaching them the basics of life was constant. Finally they could walk, talk, eat, dress themselves, and use the potty. The terrible twos was a daily battle with stubborn toddlers, but little did we know the worst was yet to come.

I would like to think my parenting skills were getting better, but the daily routine of raising three children seemed to come right out of the comic strips. Many times I felt like the characters portrayed in them, especially when the comic strip revealed a situation we just experienced. This happened more than once. I started cutting the cartoons from the newspaper and magazines that represented our lives. I have quite a collection. I never realized how long my parenting skills would be needed, and I was starting to feel overwhelmed. On occasion I would go out with my friends for a break from our daily routine. My friend and I planned to go bowling. She arrived early and the children were just finishing an orange sherbet treat. I offered her a cup of coffee while waiting for my babysitter. When she got up, I noticed an orange sherbet stain on the back of her slacks. I did not tell her because I was afraid she would not want to go bowling with the stain. I was so desperate. I just had to get out of the house for a while. This is what I had been reduced to.

One day while I was driving my children home from school my perfect daughter was acting like a total obnoxious brat. She would not stop tormenting her little sister and brother. Before long all three were unbearable. I stopped the car and told the perfect child to get out and walk home. We were fifty feet from home, but she got the message. If someone would have told me when she was a year old that someday I would be stopping my car and putting out my perfect child, I would never have believed them. Who would have thought this perfect parent would be kicking this perfect child out of the car? My perfect parent skills were disappearing significantly.

Maureen was ten years old and kept begging us to let her babysit her six-year-old sister and four-year-old brother. So one afternoon, Tom and I went a couple of blocks down the street and gave her the phone number where we would be. We were only gone a few minutes when we got a call from Maureen. She was calling from her bedroom and hysterically howled "The bread drawer is open! Someone is in the house and opened the bread drawer!" Tom and I went home immediately, which took less than a minute. They were all upstairs locked in the girls' bedroom. We walked into the kitchen and looked at the bread drawer. It was partially open. They kept insisting that someone must have broken in and opened the bread drawer because it was never left open. We checked the bread drawer and all the bread and buns were still there. Tom checked the whole house and assured them no one was there. To this day they ponder over how the bread drawer opened.

This was the start of the bread drawer mysteries. Later, I noticed a crack on the front left side of the drawer. Apparently, someone was using the drawers as a step to climb up on the sink to reach the higher, off-limit cupboards for snacks. No one owned up to climbing on the bread drawer. They were all grown and well into their twenties when some stains mysteriously appeared on the varnished wood of the bread drawer over the holidays. Apparently, someone spilled gin or vodka and it splashed on the bread drawer and removed the varnish. Of course, no one owned up. So we now have three unsolved bread-drawer mysteries.

We all took a trip to the mall for some last-minute Christmas shopping. The children were going to pull their money together and buy presents. I told them to meet me at the fountain in an hour. After a while they tracked me down and excitedly shouted, "A lady stole our gold earrings. We bought them in the card shop and the cashier gift wrapped them in gold foil paper with a gold ribbon. After we left the store we discovered the cashier didn't put our package into our bag. We went right back into the store and the lady that was behind us took it because she had the box in her bag. So we followed her and then came to get you." I asked, "What lady?" They answered, "Follow us." They hurried down the hall and pointed to a lady sitting in the center of the mall and yelled, "There she is. She is the one who stole them." By this time, I was caught up in their excitement and my mother hen instincts kicked in to protect my chicks. They had me convinced that this woman had taken their package. I boldly went over to her and tactfully asked, "Were you just at the card shop?" She replied, "Yes." I asked, "Did the sales clerk put a gift wrapped package into your bag by mistake. She answered, "No." The kids retorted, "There is our package in your bag." Sure enough the gift wrapped with gold foil paper and a gold ribbon was in her bag. She replied, "I bought silver earrings and had them gift wrapped." The children insisted it was their package containing their gold earrings. She offered to open the package and show them the silver earrings that she bought. I suddenly realized I was in the middle of the mall accusing this strange lady of stealing. How would I prove that she stole their earrings? How could I make her give them back? We came this far and she did not back down. Reluctantly, I said, "Never mind." We went back to the card shop to see if someone turned in the package or if the saleslady found the package. She remembered waiting on the children (I am sure they left a lasting impression), but she didn't remember the lady after them. She said, "We wrap gold earrings in gold paper with a gold ribbon and silver earrings in silver paper with a silver ribbon." The lady had their earrings! We went out into the hallway and the lady was nowhere to be seen.

Disciplining the children was a constant challenge; I endlessly followed the grueling looney trail when I had to come up with new discipline tactics. I knew what they were going to do before they did it. If something was broken or spilled, I could tell who did it by just looking at them. I bellowed, "Who parked this bike in the middle of the driveway? Who left the lights on? Who left their shoes in the middle of the floor?" When I knew exactly who did it.

I tried to teach them there were consequences to their actions, but as hard as I tried they still continued their mischievous behavior. They slammed the back door. I waited until they got to their destination and then called them back home to open and shut the door properly twenty-five times. They would leave their bedroom lights on and go to the neighbors. I would wait until they were engaged in their play and then call them home to shut off the lights. They threw dirty clothes on the floor in the cellar way instead of taking them to the cellar. I would make them pick up the dirty clothes, carry them to the cellar, put them into the laundry basket, and come upstairs. Then I had them go to the cellar, get the dirty clothes, come back upstairs, set them down in the cellar way, and repeat the cycle twenty-five times. If Marty was around, he would keep count since he never had this consequence because of his neatness. He tremendously enjoyed counting for the girls and they tremendously hated it so it added to their punishment. The girls would not do their chores, even when I resorted to getting them out of bed at midnight in the cold of winter to take the trash cans to the curb. The punishment did not even faze them. The next week on trash day, they went to bed without taking the cans to the curb. These same behaviors were repeated day after day in spite of the consequences and disciplines. The door is constantly slammed, lights are left on, dirty clothes are thrown into the cellar way, and the trash is piling up. Why? Why?

Marty always did his chores and his room was always neat, but he was kind of a menace to the neighbors and I frequently received phone calls from them. We got to know all the neighbors quite well. I was so elated when a neighbor came knocking and complained that someone had smashed all the tomatoes in his garden. I happily announced, "Well it wasn't Marty because he is in West Virginia visiting his aunt." I am sure some of his buddies committed the crime, and without a doubt if he was home he would have been involved.

Tom and I had different ideas about parenting and disciplining the children as they got older. Whenever there was any kind of commotion, whoever was around lost their privileges and was grounded. This was his method of discipline. He wouldn't listen to the problem. This would result in unhappy children, especially the innocent bystander and the victim. Later, he would grab his golf clubs and say on his way out the door, "Kids behave and listen to your mother." Yeah right, as if that was going to happen. I was stuck with enforcing the harsh, unfair discipline with these three grounded, no-privileged children many times.

When we all went out to eat, it was nothing but bickering and chaos since Tom would say to the children, "Where do you want to eat?" Of course each child picked a different restaurant and then the arguments would start. Tom would get annoyed at the confusion and go where he wanted, and it usually wasn't anywhere they suggested. Finally, I got the children together and pleaded, "When your father asks you where you want to eat just tell him, 'Wherever you want to go is all right with us.' DO NOT SUGGEST A RESTAURANT!! You know the three of you always end up arguing and he always goes where he wants anyway. So please stop naming restaurants! Please let's stop this insanity! Then later I will take you where you want to eat." One problem solved; 99,999 more to resolve.

Teaching them simple basic skills such as closing doors, turning out lights, how to behave in a car, and picking up after themselves was frustrating, especially when they knew how and wouldn't. However, knowing is half of the battle. Call it defiance, power struggle or just plain lazy, whatever it was; I felt that I did my job well. It was disturbing when I thought, "If they are not responding to these little chores, how can I move on to bigger chores such as doing laundry, cooking, and housework? Should I even attempt? Yes, I will! It is my job!"

The early and middle years were stressful, and we got through them without too much incident. They were getting older and we thought it would be easier. But it wasn't. Oh, how we weren't prepared for three teenagers and will Marty ever stop terrorizing the neighborhood? There were so many issues that needed our judgment and attention. How can two cartoony parents handle three teenagers when one hasn't matured past twelve and lives by logic that only he understands?

Now to describe these three teenagers, the words dim-witted, foolish, ridiculous, and self-centered come to mind. They were constantly testing my patience and parenting skills. These teens were starting to show their cartoony heredity by acting foolish and looking the part. I didn't have a problem with the new styles the teens wore, but I drew the line with clothes that were full of holes, faded out, or looked like someone threw a bottle of bleach on them. I refused to buy these overpriced imperfect clothes that the teens called cool and in-style. I called them rejects. However, if they couldn't live without these flawed styles, I paid the price for a normal pair of jeans and they would have to pay the extra charge for the holes and splattered bleach.

There was a time when we had to threaten them to take a shower; now, we have to beg them to get out of the shower. For the life of me I can't understand why you would take a shower before going jogging. I asked Tom, "Their demands, their wants, their needs, how do we know?" He replied with some of his parenting logic, "We just have to outsmart them."

I was driving Maureen to school one morning. I glanced over at her and she was leaning against the back of the seat with her legs straight. I asked, "Why are you leaning in the seat like that?" She answered, "I can't bend my legs because I don't want to put wrinkles in my jeans." I just looked at her and wondered, "Are you planning to stand in school all day?"

Maureen and I went shopping and she could not find a top for her jeans. After looking in every clothing store in the mall and passing by many beautiful tops I asked, "What exactly are you looking for? There are so many nice tops?" She answered, "I want to match the top with the thread in the seams of my jeans."

Occasionally, Maureen and some of her friends wore their clothes backwards. They looked comical, especially when they put their hooded jackets on backwards with the hoods up. They were definitely cartoon characters as they staggered along trying to find their way out the backdoor.

Maureen wanted a pair of shoes with high heels. I was not in favor of the shoes, since I felt she was so young and the high heels would be bad for her legs and weren't practical. She begged and begged, so I told her, "At your next doctor appointment, I will ask him about the high heels, and if he approves of the shoes you can get them." A few weeks later at her doctor's appointment, I asked about the high heels and the doctor stated, "High heels are not good for *anyone* to wear." So problem solved. However, I compromised and got her a pair with a medium heel. Later, I was in the backyard talking to a neighbor and Maureen came running across the backyard in her new shoes and *splat* she fell flat on the ground with her face smashed into the grass. Oh, the things I wanted to say but didn't.

I was amazed at what they argued about. One afternoon, Maureen was sitting on the patio eating a sandwich and chips. Lora went over and took a chip off of Maureen's plate. Maureen angrily shouted, "Stop taking my chips!" I asked her, "Why does it matter if she took a chip? There is a whole bag of chips in the kitchen." Maureen remarked, "I counted out just enough chips for my sandwich."

Lora used Maureen's perfume and Maureen was furious. When I questioned Maureen, "Why can't she use your perfume?" Maureen shouted, "It is my smell! She took my smell!" Just recently Lora used some of her own daughter's perfume and she told Lora, "Mom that is my smell. You took my smell." I hope Lora finds her own smell soon!!

One morning Maureen and Lora were arguing over clothes. One yelled, "That is my top! Take it off!" The other bellowed, "Then take off my jeans!" They kept arguing back and forth. Finally, Tom shouted some of his fashion logic, "That is enough! From now on, if it fits wear it." They immediately ran to his closet.

One morning I went for my sneakers and they were gone. All that was left on the shoe rack was some worn-out shoes. I suddenly realized that my daughters and I wore the same size shoe. The next day, the same thing happened. So I went to the shoe store and bought a pair of sneakers. The next morning they were gone. It appeared that the first one to leave the house got the best pair of shoes. This went on for a while until I went to the shoe store and found a salesperson that was the closest in age to a teenager and declared, "I want a pair of sneakers that a teenager would not want to be seen in and would rather go barefoot than wear." She looked at me and acknowledged, "Gotch ya." Then she went into the back storeroom and brought out a pair of sneakers just for me. The next morning when I went for my sneakers, they were sitting right where I left them the night before.

Each of the girls received a camera for Christmas and every chance Marty got he would sneak the cameras and hold them to his face and take a close-up picture of himself. There were many close-up pictures of their sweet brother when the girls developed their film. They would be furious. They hid their cameras, but he always found them and took his picture. These close-ups definitely reveal a looney tune character.

The girls were constantly joining book or music clubs. The concept behind joining these clubs is you receive six free books or 8-track tapes. Then you are required to purchase one item a year. They send you one a month, and if you don't want what they send all you have to do is send it back. Otherwise, you have to keep it and pay for it. This was the gimmick. Needless to say, they never sent them back so they had to pay for many books and 8-track tapes they didn't want. I am happy to say many of the books and tapes they purchased were my style of reading and music. Thanks to the girls, I have enjoyed Helen Reddy, Robert Goulet, and John Denver's 8-track tapes. I tormented them daily singing "I Am Woman" with Helen Reddy, "Country Roads" with John Denver, and every Christmas Robert Goulet accompanied me singing Christmas songs while I was preparing goodies for our party. I can only hope they learned a lesson.

One summer the girls arrived home from visiting their aunt. They weren't in the door an hour when they started arguing over the pictures they had taken. They wanted the same pictures. They squabbled for quite a while. Finally, I intervened and told them they had better settle down and solve the problem or I would. I yelled several more warnings; however, they just continued to argue. Lora shouted, "I took this picture!" Maureen answered, "But I paid for the film." Lora declared, "But I paid for the developing." Maureen protested, "But this is my friend." Then their argument escalated into yelling and grabbing. Finally I solved their dilemma. I walked into the room, took all the pictures, tore them in half, and gave each child half of all the pictures and shouted, "Now you each have half of the pictures." They just gaped in quiet disbelief.

They were constantly challenging my parenting skills. They would cling to the rare occasion when I was wrong and accused them unjustly. Many times when I disciplined them, they would bring up that one occasion as if that was going to make a difference.

When they accused me of having favorites, I told them, "I have no favorites. I lost each one of you." I reminded Lora about the time I dropped her off at preschool and forgot to go pick her up. I was outside doing yard work so I didn't hear the telephone when the preschool called. The teacher knew where we lived, so she dropped her off on her way to bowling. I reminded Maureen about the day I left her at school. After school, I went to pick up her and a few neighborhood kids. The car filled with kids and I drove off. Later, I discovered that she wasn't in the car. Then I reminded Marty about the time I lost him in the mall. We decided to split up and meet at the fountain in an hour. So Lora and I turned and went in one direction, and Marty and Maureen went in another direction. Later, when we met at the fountain, I saw Maureen but no Marty. I asked her where he was and she answered, "I thought he was with you." Apparently, Marty went in a direction by himself. Before I had a chance to panic I heard on the loud speaker, "We have a lost little boy named Marty. Will his parents come to the office?" I told them that I had no favorites and that I tried to get rid of each one, but it didn't work out. Seriously, though, before I had children I would hear stories about parents losing their children or leaving them somewhere and forgetting to pick them up and wonder, "How could they do that?" Now I know!

They complained our dentist wasn't very competent, since they never needed any dental work. Most of their friends had fillings and braces. They could not understand why they never had any cavities or braces. It never occurred to them it was genetics, eating properly, and proper care of their teeth. They were all in their twenties before they had their first cavities.

They were looking at pictures from their childhood and after a while they asked, "How could you let me dress like that?" I answered, "You would have looked worse than that if I would have allowed you to dress how you really wanted."

Before long I observed them taking a familiar course. With both parents traveling down the looney tune trail at a fast pace, it was foreseeable that sooner or later the children would start wandering down the looney trail with experiences of their own.

Maureen played basketball for our church girls' team. At one of the games, the score was tied with just seconds left to play. Maureen intercepted the ball, dribbled down the court, jumped up into the air, aimed for the rim, threw the ball, and swished two points. She looked just like a pro. Everyone from the other team was cheering and excited. Her coach shouted, "Nice shot, Maureen. However, next time shoot in our basket." She shot in the other team's basket and the other team won thanks to Maureen's two points.

One evening the three brave teens were in the living room watching a horror movie. The main scary character was a toy baby doll that came to life and terrorized the people. I got a doll from the attic and snuck outside and put the doll up to the window and knocked on the glass. You should have heard the screams of horror coming from the courageous teens.

The day after the prom Maureen, her date, and some of their friends went to Cook Forest. They went hiking and canoeing. Later that day, everyone came home except Maureen's date. For some reason, he was left at Cook Forest. His mother had to go and get him. Why, I don't know to this day.

When Maureen got her first part-time job at a small sub shop, she would treat herself to a new shirt every payday. One day she came to me and declared, "I don't like how you wash my clothes; I am going to wash my new things by hand." I answered, "Great!" One sunny day she hand-washed her shirts and hung them on the line. She kissed them and announced to me, "Now that is how to wash!" Later she came running into the house and screamed, "Look what a bird did to my new shirt!"

We drove Maureen an hour and fifteen minutes to college on Wednesday. She was so excited because this was the first time she was on her own. We unpacked the car with all her college necessities and helped her settle in. Then we took her to dinner and then back to her dorm where we hugged and whispered our sad goodbyes. She even hugged her little brother and sister, and they hugged her back. On the way home I felt a little guilty when I envisioned some peace and quiet with no more sisters quarreling. Lora had the whole bedroom to herself, the bathroom, and all the clothes. Friday we were relaxing in the living room enjoying the peace and quiet when Maureen darts into the house shouting, "Surprise!" She hopped a ride home with a friend who lived in the area. She wasn't even gone two full days. I didn't even get a chance to miss her.

Years later, when Maureen was teaching in Florida, she flew home for Christmas. We went to the airport and waited for her to get her luggage. Tom put her yellow suitcase into the trunk and we headed to Sharpsville. She was very excited about her job and talked all the way home. When she started to unpack, she noticed presents and other items in the suitcase that were not hers. Apparently, this was not her suitcase. At the airport it never occurred to her that someone else might have an identical model. She called a number she found in the luggage. Maureen said, "I will take your suitcase to the airport tomorrow." The girl was not very happy and was rude to Maureen. She couldn't figure why the girl was so angry since she was going to return her suitcase the next day.

Tom shows his cartoony side and bizarre logic in everything he does. His parenting experiences have proved this over and over. It's no wonder everyone is turning into a cartoon character with all this drama. As the kids got older, we traveled down the looney family trail together. I lost track of how many times we went into church and when the first person stopped to go into a pew, everyone would bump into each other. It kind of reminded me of the five stooges.

We were vacationing at the beach in Ocean City, which is just a few miles from Atlantic City. The guys spent a day at the casinos and the gals babysat and prepared supper, and the next day the gals spent the day at the casinos and the guys babysat and prepared supper.

Maureen, Lora, and I arrived early in the morning at a casino so we could be one of the first 100 people to get an American flag. We each received one when we entered the casino. The flags were all numbered and there was a possibility of one of us winning $500 at a drawing later in the day. Richard Simmons was going to be there in the afternoon, and we planned to work out with him for a while. We decided to gamble while waiting for Richard to arrive. We noticed some machines called the Sizzler, so we played them since Richard exercised to a song with the same name in one of his videos. I was sitting between the girls and every time one of us won we would get up and run around our chair swinging our American flags in the air shouting, "Sizzle."

After a while, the girls announced, "We have to go now. It's time to work out with Richard." I didn't want to leave, since I was really sizzling on my machine. Finally I gathered my winnings and followed them. We ran into Richard, who was dressed like an American flag, in the hall. He just arrived so we decided to follow him since we were going to a room to work out with him. So off we went down the hall, following him with our American flags in hand. As we were walking with Richard, more and more people joined us. Richard stopped at a stage and someone started filming him for a commercial. We gathered around the stage with the other people to watch. Then Richard announced, "I need some people up here with me." He started picking people to come up on stage. We thought for sure he would pick us since we were the first to join him in the hall. Then Richard looked at Maureen, and she thought she was being called up to be on stage and yelled, "Yahee!" She swung her American flag in the air and started toward the stage. Then Richard says, "Can she have your flag?" He pointed to one of the ladies on stage that didn't have a flag. At the same time he said this to Maureen, I instantly put my flag behind my back. She quickly jerked her flag down and shouted, "No!" Richard then gives Maureen a gasping noise and scolded her, "Well that just wasn't very nice!" Lora then jumps forward up to the stage with her American flag, telling him, "Here Richard, you can have my flag." He took Lora's flag and gave it to the lady who didn't have one. Then Lora turns to Maureen and gloats while saying, "I think Richard just said you weren't very nice!" Maureen sadly replied, "Yeah, he did!" Then a picture was taken of the ladies with Richard waving their American flags in the air while we watched. Hey, we got up early and left the condo just so we could be one of the first hundred to get a flag. It was not easy. This was quite a feat with three husbands and five kids underfoot while we were getting ready. Maureen and I were not going to give up our flags. By the way, our flag's number didn't win the contest.

Later when we told the story to the guys, Tom stated some of his sympathetic logic, "He shouldn't have called anyone up on stage without a flag." This is one of the few times we all agreed with his logic.

We were going to visit Tom's sister in Akron for the day. Maureen and the grandchildren were home from Texas, so we decided to take two cars since there were too many of us to fit into one. Of course, Tom was ready to leave before the rest of us and was trying to hurry us along. He was taking the boys, and the girls were going with me. Finally we were ready, and Maureen asked Tom for directions. As he started up the road, he stated with some of his traveling logic, "You don't need directions; just follow me." So we started up the street behind him. By the time we got to the top of the street, he was gone out of sight. He was driving a beige Cadillac and before long we saw a beige car and proceeded to follow it. He turned onto a side street in Sharon, and Maureen asked, "Why is he turning down this street?" I answered, "He is probably taking a short cut; just follow him." Then he turned to the right down another street; we followed him to the end of the street and he pulled into some tall grass and parked. While he was getting out of the car, Maureen rolled down her window and yelled, "What are you parking for?" Just then she realized the fellow she was yelling at was not her father. Thank goodness, he didn't notice her. The two of us realized at the same time that we were following the wrong car. We both roared with laughter and she put her car into reverse and backed up the street and turned around. Now we realized we were on our own. I had been to Tom's sister's home a few times, but she lives about an hour and a half away on some curving roads in Ohio. I have mentioned before I have no sense of direction. Nevertheless, I got us close, and we called his sister for directions the rest of the way. Tom was already there relaxing on the deck drinking a beer unconcerned about our troubles. When we finally arrived Maureen asked, "Why didn't you wait for us?" He answered with some of his sarcastic logic, "You're here, aren't you?"

One afternoon, Maureen and I were going shopping so we stopped to get a light lunch to tide us over until supper. We ordered drinks and decided to split a cheeseburger, since it was a half-pounder and she wanted a salad and I decided on soup. The waitress overheard us and announced, "That will be $3 extra if you want to split the meal. I declared, "I never heard of such a thing." Maureen proclaimed, "Let's leave." She stated you have to pay for your drinks. I had a cola and Maureen had water. We got up and tried to keep a low profile as we went to the register to pay for a cola. The cashier couldn't get the computer to work so she couldn't take my money; meanwhile, the manager came out and asked us why we were leaving. We explained we wanted to split the cheeseburger, and he revealed if we would have ordered soup or salad we could split it without an additional cost. I said, "We were going to, but the waitress didn't give us a chance to order." Again he stated, "You can split your meal at no extra cost as long as you order soup and salad." We answered, "No thanks, we are going." Finally the girl got the register to work and rang up my cola. I paid for it and we left.

We went to another restaurant and were still huffing and puffing when we sat down at a table. We asked the waitress if we could split a meal and she answered, "Yes." We were explaining our experience at the previous restaurant and the manager overheard and came over and talked to us. He asked, "Are you going back to the other restaurant?" We both answered, "No, never." He revealed, "I try to keep my customers happy. I don't charge for sharing meals. I figure maybe next time you may buy a steak dinner." When the waitress came back to take our order, we ended up not sharing a meal.

When I go to Texas to visit Maureen, we always take a day and go to a town where the "well to do" hang out. We pretend we are rich for the day. We visit the stores and marvel at the outrageous prices. We always find some little trinket we like and can afford. In the parking lot of a swanky restaurant where we were going for lunch, I overheard someone say, "Well it was only $100,000." When we entered the restaurant a couple of gentlemen in suits held the door open and I turned and told Maureen, "Well it only cost $100,000." She asked, "What?" I repeated myself and again she asked, "What?" By this time we were through the door and I whispered, "We're rich, remember?" She had forgotten for a brief time but composed herself and got back into character.

Maureen had a basal cell skin cancer removed from her lip. She had an appointment with a plastic surgeon in this high-class town, so I stated, "We have to get serious now and act civilized." While we were waiting to see the doctor a man came out of one of the examining rooms and walked toward the doors as he was leaving. He smashed his face into the glass door and left a large imprint smear of his face on the glass. I was struggling to keep my composure when Maureen leaned over and whispered, "I hope he didn't just get a nose job." Then we both lost our self-control and exposed our roots.

One Christmas, Maureen and Leah, her daughter, flew home from Texas. We were at Lora's and Leah brought her flute so Maureen asked Lora's daughter, Hattie, to get her flute and play for us. After the first song, Maureen and Lora got caught up in the moment remembering when they used to play their flutes at Christmas and sat beside them and requested a picture. The girls played another song and another and another and another and then Maureen asked them to stop. They ignored her request and continued playing—somewhat like Maureen and Lora ignored our requests for them to stop playing on Christmas Eve a few years ago. Finally, Lora shouted, "Enough!" They continued to play until Lora could stand it no more and screamed, "Out! Get up to your room! Both of you! Out! Out!!" Oh the spirit of Christmas! Don't they remember they did the exact same thing at their ages?

Tom is comical when he travels down the "Papa" trail; three incidents come to mind when he was in charge of the five. The first was when he took a nap with grandson, Emory, and the littlest grandchild, Hattie, cut the Barbie's hair and all the clothes. The second story was when we came home and he didn't know where one was. The third story occurred in the summer when we found them at the end of our dead-end street playing in the weeds.

When Emory was five years old and getting ready to start kindergarten, Tom told him, "I will take you out to eat anywhere you want to go and then I will take you shopping for a toy." Emory stayed overnight and got up bright and early waiting for Papa to take him out to eat and shopping for his toy. Just before they left, Tom got a phone call about a relative who had come to town and wanted to talk to him about some of the family. She was working on her family tree. So we went to his mother's to meet the relative. Tom told Emory to watch television for a few minutes while he visited with the relative, and then they would go out to eat. Now this few minutes turned into a few hours. Emory was very patient and finally Tom was ready to go. He suggested a restaurant in Sharon that he thought Emory would like. Emory answered, "Okay." So we went downtown Sharon to the restaurant and while we were walking across the parking lot someone sitting on the patio yelled, "Hey, Tom." It was our friends from Florida. We stopped and talked for a while. Then we joined them for lunch. Again, Emory was patient while we talked for a couple of hours. Then we got into the car and headed to the toy store. I told Emory that today turned out to be Papa's day and that we would take him out another day that would be his day. Disappointed, he declared, "Everyday is Papa day!" The more I think about it, he is absolutely right.

Every summer there is always a mystery to be solved. With five grandchildren of assorted ages running around the house for a month, there is bound to be some disasters. You would think with six adults around, they would be closely supervised. Most of the time they were, but on that rare occasion when everyone was sitting on the deck and patio thinking someone else was looking after the children, they took advantage of the freedom.

Something was always getting broken and grandson #2 admitted to breaking the lamp, vase, and timer. But one summer, Tom noticed the computer had a big scratch on the monitor. When he questioned "the five" no one knew anything about it and all the evidence pointed to grandson #2. So Tom announced with some of his Papa logic, "Friday at 1:00 PM we will have a trial. He appointed a prosecution lawyer, a defense lawyer, a judge, and he was the jury. Grandson #2 was found guilty on circumstantial evidence.

Another summer, all his herbs were cut off to the roots. He held another trial and again all the evidence pointed to #2 grandson. He was the only one who didn't have an alibi for when the crime was committed.

All the grandkids have a different perspective of the trials. This is what Hattie wrote about the trials: "Papa always had a mystery for me and Leah to solve and we always put Nathan on trial. Emory is always Nathan's lawyer when we were at the trial we had another mystery to solve. But me and Nathan admitted to breaking the timer. Grandpa was always the judge and he would always ask Leah and I why we always put Nathan on trial every year. Nathan's innocent we are all convinced it was one of the adults that cut the herbs. Nathan was the only one that didn't have an alibi."

Before long I think the grandchildren will be putting their grandpa on trial, since he torments and scares them with his stories of the walking leg, just like he scared his own children years before. He turns his eyes inside out and makes all sorts of scary faces to go along with the stories.

Lora had a Halloween party and the grandchildren helped decorate the back patio with pumpkins, black cats, skeletons, ghosts, witches and Dracula. The children were having a good time playing in the haunted room, and the adults were enjoying themselves in the living room. That is until Tom went into the patio. Suddenly, all the children came running out of the patio screaming and ran straight to their mothers crying and didn't leave their sides for the rest of the evening. They wouldn't go back out to the patio regardless of what anyone said or how much comfort their mothers gave them.

Later, I noticed Emory and some of the children going upstairs and when they came down I noticed them giggling. I went over to see what they were up to. They remembered the only thing that scared Papa was snakes, so they found a play snake in their playroom and wanted to scare him. I went outside with them and they snuck into Papa's car and put the snake on the steering wheel. When he was ready to go home, all the children went to the window to watch his reaction when he discovered the snake on the steering wheel. He got into the car and started it up and never noticed the snake. When he put the car into drive, I had to tell him since I was afraid we would get into a wreck when he discovered the snake. I showed him the snake and told him, "React for the children. They are watching through the window." So he pretended he was afraid of the snake; however, he wouldn't touch it. I had to remove it from the steering wheel. I couldn't resist wiggling it toward him and getting a real reaction of him being scared of the snake. All the children laughed and felt they got revenge.

It amazes me how many times I pick up a magazine or newspaper and there is a cartoon strip that portrays situations that we just experienced. We have definitely passed our cartoony genes onto the next generation, and I suppose they will do the same. As they journey through life, I am sure they will continue to venture on similar trails; I know Tom and I will be there. Sometimes we travel alone, but many times we all journey together on that inevitable cartoon trail.

*Guess I was being a little annoying again since my older cousin
has a choke hold on me.*

Liz started to look like a cartoon character as early as second grade.

My precious doves are sitting on the coffee table where they were to stay forever.

The girls are enjoying another of Dad's vacations through the scenic countryside.

Tom is resting on a fence in Watkins Glen.

Tom is sorting the first pile of his important papers.

*Not listening again. This is where Tom placed the air conditioner after I
asked him several times to put it along the side so
I can get to the back of the attic.*

Marty's expression explains my baking. The pineapple upside-down cake is splattered to the right of the pan.

When I say plants have a short life span under my care I'm not joking. Even the leaves fall from my artificial plant.

Tom is passing on his Lally logic to Marty.

Splat!!

Dismount.

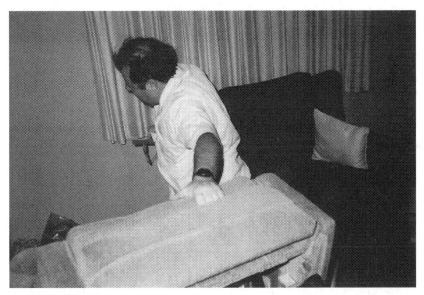

Hang in there. Someday you'll master the recliner.

Lora is holding a cabbage patch doll, Emory. This was her sweet sixteen birthday present. She named her first child after the doll.

Tom and I are opposites. He relaxes at the noisy coffee shop.

I relax at the quiet park.

Grandpa was looking after the grandchildren. Nice job with Emory.
However, where are the other four grandchildren and what are they doing?

Grandpa scared all the little children at the Halloween party. They wouldn't leave their parent's side for the rest of the party.

Every summer when the five grandchildren are visiting things get broken or destroyed. Last summer Tom's herbs were destroyed. Tom held a trial to discover the guilty grandchild.

Leah and Hattie entertained the family at Christmas. Maureen and Lora reminisced about a time not so long ago when they entertained the family on Christmas with their flute playing.

The poolside room Tom reserved so I could sit on the balcony and write while he was at meetings. My poolside room was boarded on all sides behind the dolphin.

Maureen edited my book at the Gaylord in Texas.

Maureen edited my book at Gervasi Vineyard in Canton.

*High tech Lal was caught using a notebook and pen.
I will low tech him yet.*

*Never thought I would be sitting here pondering over what shade of white
paint to paint the kitchen and living room.*

6

Technology

My technology journey is definitely a sea of confusion as I float down the cartoon waterway. I feel threatened and inadequate in a rapidly changing world. Technology is moving too quickly for me to keep up with, and I am still trying to grasp speed dial. Everywhere I go there are electronic devices with flashing lights and far-fetched monotone voices. I grow older and slower while everything around me is newer and faster and too technical for me to understand; I just don't think that way. I typed a story on our first computer and saved it on a disk. A few days later, I took my story off the disk to add something. I messed up and it disappeared. Then I retyped the whole story all over again and saved it on the disk. Later, I took my story off the disk to add something. I messed up again and it disappeared. Then I retyped the whole story all over again and saved it on the disk. This cycle continued with everything I typed for over a year until I was in a discussion about computers with some friends. I discovered my information was still on the disk even though I took it off. I didn't comprehend that my original information was still on the disk and all I had to do was go back into the disk and get it again when I lost it in "Computer Land." It was still on the disk even though I took it off. WHAT!! How can that be?

Technology and my brain aren't in sync. I led a modest, frugal and very practical existence the first fourteen years of my life, since I was the last of the outhouse, icebox, scrub board, and winger washer generation. Our home had no indoor plumbing; we walked to a neighbor's well every day, and with his hand pump we pumped water into buckets and carried them home. I remember going to the well for water when I was so young all I could carry was half a bucket. Water was heated in big pans on the gas stove for dishes, baths and laundry. Our heat came from a pot-belly coal stove in the living room. We didn't have a telephone or television; for entertainment, we listened to the radio and played records on the phonograph. Twice a month when Dad got paid, he took us to the movies and we stayed and watched the films twice. My low-tech thinking was apparent when I wondered how the actors did the exact same thing in the second movie as they did in the first. I would watch the first movie closely and find things that were impossible to do exactly the same way again. However, in the next movie they did it exactly the same, even the animals. I was mesmerized, bewildered, and amazed.

My technical intelligence hasn't improved much since then. I received many wedding gifts I didn't know the name of or how to use. The appliances were difficult for me to operate since I was used to simple, uncomplicated utensils that were handed down from mother to daughter. I had difficulty understanding the concept of a separate large bulky electrical appliance for everything. I struggled with the mixer, blender, waffle iron, electric skillet, and electric can opener; these appliances had to be disassembled after every use and cleaned. They were certainly a waste of electricity, space, and time. My cozy warm blankets from my bed were replaced with an electric blanket. It was uncomfortable and I could actually feel the wires. It came with a warning label that haunted me into a terror of electrocution. The electric blanket had to go. I had a garage sale and went back to my warm cozy blankets, spoons, cast iron skillet, and a simple can opener. My mother-in-law had an old wringer washer in the cellar, which she gave me to use. I felt that an automatic washer and dryer were a waste of electricity and water. Eventually, I got an automatic washer and dryer. Currently, I use my automatic washer; however, over the last several years, I haven't used my dryer at all.

A while back, I felt like a cartoon character when I went to rent VCR tapes when much to my surprise the shelves were filled with DVDs. I thought I was in the twilight zone. I asked the salesperson, "What happened to all the VCR tapes?" She answered, "There are a few on the shelves in the back of the store, but we have mostly DVDs." Of course, Tom had a DVD player but it was hooked up to his computer. I didn't want to sit in the computer room and strain my eyes looking at a smaller screen when I had a comfortable couch in the living room and a bigger screen and a VCR. I was satisfied with my VCR tapes until they stopped selling them, and eventually I relented and purchased a DVD player and DVDs.

My music cycle has been a difficult journey through technology. I cringe when I think of all the devices I have purchased with my hard earned allowances and pay from my first job, only to be replaced with something new in just a few years when they quit making them. I have come from cranking my phonograph to pushing a button on my CD player. That's as far as I'm going! I refuse to go any further in the music world. Here the cycle ends for me! I'm just too weary.

Before I figured out the difference between CDs and DVDs they came out with new ways to listen to music and watch movies; however, I am not advancing any further into the technology world. It took me a long time to figure out the difference between a CD and a DVD because they looked the same. I kept getting them mixed up. I know a CD just plays music and a DVD is a movie. I bought a three pack of music CDs; however, it was really two CDs and one DVD. I didn't know this. For the longest time, I kept putting the DVD into the CD player and it wouldn't work so I thought the one CD was defective. Why do they mix a DVD in with CDs? I was in the music department purchasing CDs not DVDs. It's no wonder I'm confused.

I am done with all the letters and numbers: 33, 45, 8-track, VCR, CD, DVD. This is as far as I am going down the alphabet and numbers trail. I am not even going to try and figure out what an iPod does. I can't even begin to communicate with the younger generation, which is so busy downloading and is very impatient; they want everything instantly. I just don't speak the language. I feel like I am entering a foreign country where I don't know the lingo.

I can't escape the prevailing conditions of meaningless, distracting, endless texts. It's an alphabet world where they are texting letters, not words, and sometimes they speak using letters, not words. The other day I was listening to a couple of the younger generation discussing a lot of abc nonsense about iPod, iPad, iPhone, and DS. I thought, "What are all those letter about? Doesn't anyone speak words anymore?" After a while of listening, I told them, "That sounds like a bunch of "BS" to me."

I can't help noticing that when a computer shuts down, people turn into helpless zombies; the sales clerks don't know what to do, and cashiers can't make change. I went to the mall to shop at a clothing store and found the store dark and the security door down. The employee was standing helplessly in front of the store. I asked him, "Why isn't the store open?" He answered, "The computer is down. I called the security guard." I waited until the security guard appeared, and he couldn't open the door either. So I left while they were pondering what to do next. A store at the mall was closed at prime time shopping because a computer was down and they didn't know how to open the door. Really?

I went to a fast-food restaurant where the lines were backed up and the employees appeared confused. When I finally got to the front of the line and ordered, the employee was frazzled and had difficulty taking my order and figuring my change. I asked, "What is the problem?" She answered, "The computer is down."

Tom and I were at a restaurant and it took forever to get our meal, even though there were only two other couples in the restaurant. When the waitress finally served our meals, she apologized, "I'm sorry for the delay. Our computers are down." I didn't understand why that could cause such a delay. Instead of entering our order into the computer all she had to do was take the paper she wrote our order on and hand deliver it to the cook. Then after the meal was prepared, he could ding a bell and the waitress could go back and get it and serve us. I don't see a problem. We ate there the whole weekend and the service never improved and we had to listen to each waitress make excuses for the poor service. "The computer is down," they all said. It amazes me how we didn't have trouble receiving good service before computers came along.

When I told Maureen about my experiences with computers down in restaurants, much to my surprise, she disclosed a recent experience, "A pizza restaurant's computer was down and they would not take my order over the phone. I asked, 'Can't you write down large pizza with pepperoni and I will come get it!' They said, "No! The computer is down.""

I called to make a doctor's appointment and the receptionist informed me, "You will have to call back later; our computer is down." I called a couple hours later, and the receptionist apologized, "The computer is still down; it just can't keep up with me." I decided to call another day. I'm so glad I didn't have an emergency.

Many times I wait while someone struggles with the computer and actually talks to it. Finally, they surrender to the computer and say, "It will just be a few minutes. I have to reboot the computer." They apologize for the long wait. I would like to "reboot" them, since all they need to do is take my check and make me an appointment in six months.

There was a small thunder shower and all twenty-four televisions in a local tavern stopped and the TV screens posted, "Searching for signal on Satellite."

So welcome to the computer world. When the computer stops, so does everything and everyone turns into zombies. I can't make appointments, stores can't open, my order can't be made, cashiers, can't make change. Wow! It wasn't any wonder that I was so frazzled about the coming of 2000! Tom wondered why I was concerned with the approaching new century. Every day the news forecast more possibilities of a total disaster, "All the computers will stop working and people will get stuck in elevators, not be able to pump gas for cars, no power for electricity or gas." We were suppose to go to Texas and visit with Maureen over Christmas, but the closer it got to the new millennium, the more paranoid I became. Finally, I refused to go to Texas.

I was so relieved there were no major disasters at the turn of 2000. However, two good things came out of my hysteria. Since we didn't go to Texas over Christmas, I told Maureen we would come in the spring and look after the grandchildren while she went on a vacation. They went to Las Vegas and had such a good time; they go back a couple times a year. Second, I have all kinds of survival equipment for a total blackout, and the greatest are the long-johns that Tom and I wear all winter. Of course, Tom wasn't concerned about all the possible disasters with the coming of the millennium. He is still my fearless leader and orders me go first when there is any sign of danger so he can respond to the emergency!

One day Tom and I were riding in the car and he declared, "Put your purse in the back seat; it is a danger to you if we get into a wreck. Actually, you shouldn't have anything in the front seat or in your pockets. It could hurt you in a car accident." I was impressed with his caring concern. Shortly after this disclosure he discovered a navigation program for his computer. We were planning to visit his sister in Michigan. He insisted I hold a heavy portable computer on my lap with the navigation so he could watch a dot moving along a line on the screen all the way to Michigan. He also swerved to the right when he leaned over to look at the computer, and the fellow he was cutting off would beep his horn. Like a dummy, I held the computer even though it was very heavy, cumbersome, and dangerous. I grew weary and struggled with his inconsistent demand of me having nothing in the front seat on one trip but then asking me to hold a heavy computer on another. I traveled this way for a few trips, then after much thought I refused to be his navigation zombie. I guess his technology comes before my safety. Now his cars are loaded with the latest technology computers that tell him everything, even where to go. There were a few times over the years when I would have liked to tell him where to go!!!

Tom's uncontrollable need for the latest cutting edge technology has always been very difficult for me to understand. I find him very annoying with his latest gadgets. When he has a gadget in his hand, he just doesn't listen! We were headed out the door to the coffee shop when Lora called and said, "I am going to drop my car off at the garage when the children get home from school. I need a ride home from the garage. My car is not going to be done till Monday. I don't need a car over the weekend, but I might need a ride to work Monday." After I repeated this to Tom, he replied, "Does this mean she will pick you up at the coffee shop?" He was playing with one of his gadgets while I was talking to him and only caught a couple words; not listening as usual.

I can't keep up with the names of all the accessories and gadgets Tom uses on a daily basis. When I need my book backed up on the computer, I say to Tom, "Will you back up my book? Here is the burgundy rectangle." He used to have a problem with the names I gave his high-tech gadgets until one day a friend came over and he overheard us discussing our husbands and their gadgets. She said,

"My husband has so many gadgets, I just refer to them as thingies." At least I describe his gadgets and don't lump them all up into one word: "Thingies." He has finally given up and doesn't get disturbed at what I call them.

Sometimes he will e-mail or text someone, and if they don't answer immediately, he will wonder all day long if they got his text. I finally say, "Pick up the phone and ask."

My journey through technology has certainty displayed some drastic transformation. I have come from the crude technology of food preservation in an icebox to my frost free fridge, from the phonograph to my CD player, from the outhouse to an indoor toilet, and from the pump at my neighbors well to indoor plumbing. I am struggling with the fast pace of technology and am about as far as I am going along the technology trail. However, among my circle of friends, I am considered high-tech! My goal is to bring Tom a few steps back. I will low-tech him *if we live long enough*.

7

Liz Logic Verses Lally Logic

Tom still lives by logic of his own creation, which long ago his friends labeled "Lally Logic," and he has been blasting me with this annoying perspective for over fifty-years. It amazes me how he comes up with some of his logic. The other day he received a letter in the mail and started to mutter some of his rambling logic, "Why did they send me this letter? Now I know, and when you know you have to think. When you don't know, you don't have to think. And now I know so I have to think." I had no idea what he said. When I inform him that his logic is exasperating and most of the time doesn't make sense, he answers, "You just need to change your thinking" and continues with the same irritating logic. I'm certainly not going to change my thinking, and I guess he's not going to change his trying logic. He uses his "Lally Logic" for every situation, and I mean every situation.

Traveling with him is always an adventure down the looney driving trail, since he never writes down addresses and won't stop and ask for directions when we are lost. Many times he doesn't have a clue where he is going; therefore, we waste time and gas driving around in circles! His absurd logic: "I'm a fireman. We don't write down addresses. I always get where I'm going." Yes, I agree that you don't have to write down an address in a small town you have lived in for sixty-nine years; however, you need to for the rest of the world.

One summer we planned a trip to the Pittsburgh Zoo, and Tom was having a little trouble finding the street where it was. After a while of driving up and down the hills of Pittsburgh, I asked Tom to stop and ask for directions. He stated his traveling logic, "No, I don't ask for directions." I said no more and continued looking out the window. However, after we passed the same waterfall flowing down a hillside for the third time, I just had to say, "You are going around in circles! You have gone past this same waterfall three times. Will you please stop and ask for directions?" He answered, "These street signs in Pittsburgh don't make sense, but I can find anyplace." I responded, "Yes, I suppose you could if you drove around long enough, but you have three restless children in the back seat who are excited about the zoo as we passed the waterfall again." You might say as a husband, Tom goes that "extra mile"! That's because he never stops to ask for directions!

While Maureen was reading over this chapter, she revealed the most ridiculous story about her dad and directions. "It was the time in South Carolina when we were going to get Brandon's hair cut at one of my friend's home who had a salon in her basement. We were going shopping afterward and wanted Dad to pick up Brandon and take him home after his hair was cut. He was going for gas and then meeting us at the salon. Dad was never at my friend's house, so I was trying to give him directions. He interrupted me, 'Never mind, I will find it.' I said, 'Really, you are just going to find someone's house in a neighborhood that you've never been to before without a street or house number?'"

The other day, he proceeded to the hospital for some laboratory tests. A few minutes later, he came back and said, "I forgot the forms." I started talking to him as he was reaching for the forms. He said, "You see, you say I don't listen to you when you talk. But you always talk to me when I'm doing something." I asked, "What are you doing?" He answered, "Getting my forms." I replied, "You can't walk, pick up a form, and listen at the same time." Then he spoke some of his ludicrous logic: "I'm not here. I already left." I stated, "That doesn't make sense. If you already left, what are you doing here?" He grasped his forms and left for the hospital again. I thought, "The day before he goes to the hospital for tests he always kiddingly says, 'Well I better study for my tests.'" Maybe he's not kidding.

Lights are a constant battle with us because he always leaves all the lights on throughout the house and I am constantly switching them off. His power logic: "It takes less power to leave them on than to switch them on and off." I fell for this logic until one night we were watching television and a program came on that was about to experiment his light theory. I made Tom a proposition: "If they discover it takes less power to leave the lights on continually, I will stop bugging you to turn the lights off. However, if they discover it takes less power to turn them on and off then you will have to turn the lights off." He agreed. The experts experimented with the light theories and the outcome was in my favor. I won! However, he came up with some more power logic to justify leaving the lights on. "I have to leave the lights on so I can see where I'm going." I thought, "You are sitting in the living room watching television for hours and the lights in the bedrooms, bathroom, kitchen, den, halls, patio, basement, and garage need to be on so you can see where you are going when you are not even in the room?" The battle of the lights continues!

While we were visiting Maureen in Texas, one evening Maureen and I decided to go shopping. We fixed supper for Tom and Maureen's three children. When we left they were still eating. We told them, "We will be home in a few hours." Four hours later, we came home and the dirty dishes and food were still on the table. When Maureen discovered the messy kitchen, she shouted, "Why aren't these leftovers in the fridge and the dishes done?" The children answered, "Well Papa was here so we thought he was going to clean up." She looked at her father and said, "Dad!" Tom replied in his excuse logic voice, "NOW MAAAAUREEEEEN! YOU KNOW I DON'T KNOW WHERE THINGS GO!" Maureen yelled, "DAD /MILK/ FRIDGE, DAD/CHEESE/FRIDGE, DAD/SALAD DRESSING/ FRIDGE, DAD/BREAD/ PANTRY, DAD/SCRAPS / TRASH, DAD/DISHES/ DISHWASHER!" Maureen looked at me and said, "Mom can you believe this?" I answered, "I live with this."

The next summer Tom flew out to Maureen's for a visit and one evening Maureen called and told me, "Last night, Dad slopped on the kitchen floor and when I noticed it, I asked him, "Why didn't you clean this up?'" He said, "I didn't spill anything." Then she said, "Dad, we are the only ones here and I haven't been in the kitchen." Mom, can you believe this? I told her, "A wise elderly woman once told me that most men never grow up past the age of twelve." She interrupted me and bellowed, "Mom, six!"

From personal experience of living with a man who doesn't act much older than a twelve year old, I am now that wise elderly woman passing on this information to the next generation. But they probably won't listen until it's too late, just like me.

The following are actual experiences we lived through and later, while reading the newspaper and magazines, I discovered the same event portrayed by cartoon characters in comic strips.

A comic strip portrayed a woman who was pleading with her husband to take down the Christmas lights since it was early spring. I experience this every year. Tom always leaves them up well into spring and when I plead with him to take them down, he states that logic I dread the most, "I'll take care of it the first chance I get." The most humiliating instance was on March 19. It was at Marty's birthday party when one of the guests noticed the lights and plugged them in and sarcastically howled, "How nice you left the Christmas lights up for Marty's birthday!" Ha Ha!

Another comic strip portrayed a knock at the door and the couple frantically straightened up the house and then answered the door. I have lost count of how many times someone called and announced, "I'll be over in a few minutes." Tom and I hurriedly throw things into the closets, drawers, and cellar way. Then calmly answer the door. We have this one down to an art form.

At one point, he had stacks of papers piled to the ceiling on the desk. Every time I asked him to sort them and throw some away, he replies with some of his paper logic, "Don't touch them. All the papers are important. I know where to look if I need to look up something important someday." My observance was every time he wanted an important paper, he couldn't find it. Finally, he relented to my pleading and started sorting. He got a bag of chips, sat on the recliner, and I brought him piles and piles of papers. The next week, a fellow in the comics was sitting on a stack of papers he was sorting. His wife's comments were a little kinder than mine. However, her life with her cartoon character was a figment of someone's imagination. My strip is real!!

I have lost track of how many times the bottom falls out of the bag Tom is carrying and everything comes crashing to the pavement. I always plead, "Please hold the bag by the bottom." His bottomless logic response, "They should make stronger bags."

Autumn was approaching so Tom put the cover on the air conditioner, and when the first gusty wind blew the cover flew into the backyard. When I told him about the cover he informed me, "Well I can't help it the wind is too strong." I replied, "Why don't all the other covers in the neighborhood blow off?" He declared with some of his windy logic, "Well the wind is stronger in our backyard."

The next stories portray his peculiar behavior and his bizarre "Lally logic" reasoning that I live with on a daily basis. Many times, when I point out an irritating behavior that I really wish he would change he replies, "I have gotten this far in life. Why should I change?" I reply, "You should change some of your logic especially when I ask for your opinion and you suggest something. Then you get angry because I don't do what you suggest. I just wanted your opinion. I didn't ask you what I should do. The key word here is opinion." His know it all logic, "I don't give opinions. If you don't want to know, don't ask."

When I can't find something and am searching all around the house, he blasts me with some of his misplaced logic, "Where was the last place you had it?" However, when he can't find something he always accuses me of putting it somewhere. "You always hide things in plain sight," he says.

When he does something wrong, he always twists it around as if it's my fault and states some of his twisted Logic when he knows perfectly well I had nothing to do with it.

Tom always assumes things instead of finding out the facts. The worst situation is he never calls ahead. For instance, when he heads out for the garage I suggest calling and making an appointment. He replies with some of his presumed logic, "I don't ask and I don't make appointments." He drives to the garage and believes the mechanics will stop what they are doing and work on his car. They never do. They make him an appointment and he has to drive back another day.

Tom always asks me a question when I am at the computer about to send an e-mail? I complain, "Don't ask me questions when I am at the computer. You know I don't do this too often, so I really have to concentrate?" His tech response, "You should be better at the computer."

I have never experienced the empty-nest syndrome since I always felt Tom was one big helpless kid that required much attention. He had three sisters and a mother who waited on him hand and foot, and this expectation extended over into our marriage. He constantly hangs his jackets over the kitchen chairs, and all his shoes eventually end up in the kitchen. When I complain, his excuse logic is, "You used to enjoy picking up after the kids."

Every day I hear a voice coming from the kitchen, "Where is the syrup?" I answer, "Why do you open the cupboard doors and always expect what you want to be right in front? Why don't you bend, stretch, or move something?" His unreasonable logic is, "Put the stuff I want in front. What I want should always be in the front." He also leaves the cupboard doors open. When I ask, "Why?" his nutty logic response is, "I have a lot on my mind so I can't be bothered with little things like shutting cupboard doors. I don't even think about it."

Every time we leave the house he impatiently paces at the door huffing and puffing trying to hurry me along while I do last-minute things to get ready instead of making sure he has everything he needs. It takes me longer to get ready since I am distracted by his bothersome presence. When I'm ready, we go outside and then I have to stand to wait for him to back the car out of the garage. Then after I get into the car he discovers he forgot something and has to go back into the house while I sit in the car and wait. I asked him, "Instead of pacing impatiently in the house, why can't you just back the car out of the garage and make sure you have everything you need? Then you can sit and play with your latest gadget while waiting for me to come out!" His impatient logic response, "Just hurry up."

On rainy or snowy days, he always manages to park by a puddle of water, mud, or a snow pile so I have difficulty getting out of the car. He responds with his caring logic when I complain, "Just stretch over it."

He takes my car when his car is low on gas. Sometimes I run out of gas backing his car out of the driveway. Then I have to get the gas can from the garage and walk to the station for gas? His thoughtless logic response when I protest, "I have so much on my mind I never think to get gas."

When I go shopping and open the trunk, his golf clubs are always in the way and take up half the space. I struggle putting my bags into the small area. When I complain to him, his selfish logic explanation, "You never know when I may have to golf; just shop for less."

Lately, parking spaces are getting smaller and Tom's vehicles are getting larger; therefore, it's difficult backing out and it's not easy to see if someone is coming down the aisle. Tom always asks me to look to see if someone is coming. The problem is, the older we get the trickier it is to turn and twist in the position to see if cars are coming. I asked Tom "Why don't you pull through the parking space so you don't have to back out?" His parking response, "If I have to put something into the trunk, it's easier." I said, "What about all the times you don't put something into the trunk? Besides you could just pull up a little if someone is parked too close to your trunk."

I could go on forever. You would think at some point he would listen to me and try to be a little more logical—and I don't mean "Lally" logical. How hard would it be for him to change? His life would certainly be less hectic and mine would be for sure. I asked Tom if I repeatedly did anything that annoyed him. Much to my surprise and without hesitation, he replied with some Lally sarcasms, "All the time. You have a peculiar 'Liz Logic' that baffles me and sometimes it's to the extreme."

"Name one annoying logic," I replied. Well much to my surprise, he blurted out a few incidences. He revealed "First thing in the morning you are attacking me with questions when I am trying to relax. You will ask me what I want for supper while I'm eating breakfast. You want me to think and I just got up."

Liz's planning logic, "I have to plan meals in advance so I have time to go to the store or thaw something from the freezer. I only ask because I care about you and want to prepare a dinner you will enjoy. I also don't understand why you want to relax when you just got up from sleeping? I do my best thinking in the morning."

Then he attacked my cleaning technique. "You polish the Formica with oil polish that's made for wood. I set a glass down and it slides across the table."

Liz's polishing logic, "All I can say is look at the kitchen table. It is forty-six years old and the stands and coffee table they are forty-two years old and look like new in spite of the wear and tear of raising three children.

Then Tom says, "After you clean a room I can't find anything and you broke the gear off my model plane hanging from the ceiling in the computer room."

Liz's cleaning logic, "When I clean a room, I put everything away where it goes. If you put something away once in a while you would know where things are. Get over that that gear, already. I don't have time to be gentle with your models. Only the sturdy survive my cleaning. You know you could dust your own models."

All of a sudden, I can't talk properly. He continues, "You start talking in the middle of a sentence and I don't know what you are talking about. You talk about six things at once and you keep changing the subject and going back and forth."

Liz's communication logic: "You don't start listening to me until you hear something interesting, then you accuse me of starting in the middle of a sentence. All six things I talk about are related subjects—one thing leads to the other and back again. I got an A in my communication class at college, so just maybe you are the one not communicating."

"By the time I start thinking about something your mind is made up," he replied.

My thinking response, "I anticipate what problems need solving so I research for days and seek out expert opinions. By the time you notice something needs thinking about, I already have the solution. That's a good thing, right?"

Then he started attacking my frugal side. "You keep switching the credit cards; I can't keep up."

Liz's thrifty logic, "The credit cards offer discounts on certain purchases. The green one has 5% on gas all the time. The blue card has 4% on gas, 3% on cinema and movie rentals, 2% on groceries and restaurants and 1% on all other purchases all the time. The other cards periodically offer 5% off gas, restaurants, groceries, hotels, and hardware stores. I just watch for the offers and that's the card we use during the promotion. If you checked the statements that came in the mail, you would see the money we get back for our purchases and the hundred dollar check attached to our bill every few months."

Perturbed, he stated, "When you go to the grocery store for just one thing, you buy a buggy full of things. Instead of buying one jar you buy ten jars."

Liz's shopping logic, "Why would I buy one at sale price and next week go to the store and buy another one at a higher price? That just doesn't make sense. I buy ten at a sale price to get me through till the next sale. I never pay full price on many items. Your spaghetti and meatball dinner tonight cost 85 cents. I purchased the sauce, pasta, tomato paste, garlic, and onion on sale, and the peppers were free from a neighbor. When the 99% fat-free ground beef is on sale, I make a large pot of meatballs and sauce. Then I freeze the extra in single servings for future dinners."

"You save aluminum cans and get pennies in return. It's a waste of time," he blurted.

Liz's can logic, "Rinsing cans in my dish water and putting them into a bag and taking it to the recycling on my way shopping is not a waste of time. Besides, if you have 99 cents you need a penny to make a $1.

"You have garage sales which are way too much work, and you disrupt my garage," he grumbled.

Liz's clutter logic, "You don't do any of the work and I enjoy them. I socialize with the neighbors, get rid of clutter, and make a little spending money. I don't see a problem."

He continued, "You won't get a dishwasher or a garbage disposal and I had to beg you to get a microwave. You hang the clothes on a line in the backyard. I rarely see you use the dryer."

Liz's appliance logic, "All of the contraptions you mentioned waste electricity and water. They are not as efficient as doing things yourself. Dishwashers are for sissies who don't want to get their hands wet. There is nothing better than the fresh smell of clothes blowing in the breeze on a warm summer day. Saving money by not buying expensive appliances and not wasting energy and water is a good thing; Right?"

Then he finds something wrong with the way I play sports, "You are not competitive."

Liz competitive logic, "I don't have to be the best. I do my best and I play the sport because I enjoy it. My goal isn't to clobber my opponent. I don't understand the satisfaction in beating your friends at a game when there are many people in this world who would bring you to your knees! You just happen not to be playing against them. I don't revel in someone's defeat."

Lastly, he attacked my punctuality. "It takes you too long to get ready to go somewhere."

Liz's promptness logic, "If I didn't have so much cleaning to do around the house and had a little help, maybe I could sit around the house in my good clothes like a certain person and always be ready to go."

I don't see any peculiar extreme thinking or behavior here. Everything he stated, I had a valid reason for doing and I either saved money, time, or resources. However, he will never see it that way. At some point one would think that we would start to agree on things after living together for so long, but we don't. The long, harrowing journey through marriage, Lally Logic, and Liz's Logic has been totally illogical. How we function is a mystery to me.

I often wonder if we were as compatible as I once thought. Where are the days when he was my magnet and I was the steel, he was the bread and I was the butter? Now I feel like I am the tin and he is the rust, I am the sunshine and he is the rain, I am the windshield and he is the bug (SPLAT)! How could we be so much alike then and now quite the opposite? Where is my starry-eyed lover with all the compassion who clung to my every word with unending interest? All of a sudden, he likes things he never revealed before, and it seems we like different things and do very little together. We are definitely two separate people and not as compatible as we were. When I asked him why he changed and that I didn't think we were compatible anymore, he replied with some of his distorted logic, "What are you talking about? We do everything together. I haven't changed and we are still compatible. I make a mess and you clean it up; I make the bills and you pay them; you cook the meals and I eat them. How could a couple be more compatible? Our home is a castle and I am the king." I asked, "Well what does that make me?" He answered with some loving logic, "You can be anything you want to be."

8

The Cartoon Characters
Vacationing

A group of our friends vacation at Cook Forest every summer and they are always talking about relaxing in cozy cabins, hiking through the trails, and peacefully canoeing down the tranquil Clarion River. Tom and I were always busy doing other things with our family and were never able to go. Finally, one summer we were free on the weekend of the trip. But it was also our anniversary weekend, and I told Tom I would rather go somewhere alone and have a relaxing romantic weekend enjoying candlelight dinners and watching the sunset. Tom said with some of his endearing logic, "What better place to chill out than at Cook Forest canoeing down the Clarion River and relaxing in a cozy log cabin with our friends. I will reserve a motel and after we spend the weekend with our friends, we can celebrate our anniversary. We will go to a romantic dinner in the cool mountain air and watch the sunset over the Clarion River." This weekend sounded a little too perfect. I felt a little suspicious; the golf weekend he took me on a couple of years ago still haunts me. So I called my friends just to make sure they were going because I wanted to avoid another devastating trip like the golf trip to the Pennsylvania Mountains. (The golf trip is in my first book *Help! I Married a Cartoon Character*)

We headed for Cook Forest early Friday morning and it was a beautiful day; the weather forecast for the whole weekend was mild. While driving through the fresh mountain air I started anticipating a peaceful weekend with our friends. I envisioned sitting by a stone fireplace in a rustic log cabin sipping on a cool glass of chardonnay while engaging in small conversation with our friends. I always enjoy listening and telling stories of the good old days. Some of these friends we knew forever; they were our classmates. As the fresh country air blew through my hair, I thought about hiking through the trails and canoeing down the tranquil Clarion River. This will be a fabulous mini-vacation. I just wanted to unwind and relax. The farther we drove into the wilderness, the more I was reminded of that dreadful golf trip Tom took me on a couple of years ago. However, this was going to be a fun weekend at a great place with some great friends so I put that horrible trip out of my mind.

Before long we reached our destination, and I could see some of our friends in the distance. There weren't any log cabins that I had envisioned in sight, just scruffy, shabby shacks. There were no comfy, cozy cabins. But I thought maybe they looked better on the inside. I was wrong! The inside was worse, with some old musty worn-out furniture and no fireplace. There would be no conversation while sipping wine around the fireplace. I asked a fellow why they weren't staying in the cabins and he said, "We like it better here because we can build a campfire and play ball in the field across the street." Out of the corner of my eye I saw a huge plastic bat and ball. I couldn't help thinking, "Oh, no! Here we go again!"

They rented two three-bedroom shacks with a pop-out couch in the living room. There were eight couples so two couples had to sleep on the pop-out couches in the living room. Since there were no volunteers, the diplomat in the crowd decided to flip a coin for the rooms. Of course, Tom and I got a pop-out couch. While we were unpacking our car, I hesitated for a moment regretting that I bought new outfits specifically for this weekend; my old clothes would have been more appropriate. I noticed some of the guys going into the woods to collect firewood for the campfire. A couple of them were former boy scouts and were reliving their scouting days. They turned into little boys quarrelling about which wood to use and how to, where to, and when to start the campfire. It was decided to wait and build the campfire since we were going out to dinner. At dinner, the guys planned the weekend events while the gals got caught up on what was happening in our lives.

After dinner, the scouts in the group proceeded to build a campfire while I sat on a log in my new outfit sipping on chardonnay. The conversation was interesting and far from quiet. However, I have to admit it was peaceful sitting around the campfire after the scouts finally got it started. Before long our friend started telling his jokes. He often entertains us on trips such as this. When he says, "I have a joke to tell you," everyone says, "Oh no, here we go again." But everyone listens because he is such a comical storyteller. He starts to tell the joke and only says a couple of words and then he laughs hysterically. Finally, he composes himself enough to speak a few more words and starts to giggle again; he rarely gets to the punch line. Everyone is in stitches watching him desperately try to tell the joke with his non-sense chatter and not really expecting him to get through the joke anyway. We were laughing so hard, there wasn't a dry eye among us. He actually thinks his jokes are funny, but we are really laughing at the fact he has never told a joke from the beginning to the end.

Around midnight, a couple decided to call it a night. They told everyone goodnight and went to bed. They had just settled in when some of the guys got a bucket of water and headed for their room. They poured the bucket of water on them and bolted out the door laughing like teenagers. The couple was wide awake now so they changed into dry clothes and came back to the campfire. Everyone sat innocently and one of the guys asked, "Why did you decide to come back to the campfire?" I'm not going to repeat what they said to him. This time they were the last to go to bed. Apparently it's a tradition with our friends to drench the first couple to go to bed. Tom and I didn't know this and neither did the soaked couple. This was one time I was glad Tom is always the last man standing.

The next morning, we all jumped into the back of a pickup truck and headed for the river to go canoeing. I was really looking forward to a peaceful relaxing ride down the calm, scenic Clarion River in the new outfit I bought especially for this adventure. As we pulled into the office parking lot, I thought, "What a beautiful day! It's perfect for a canoe ride." The guys went into the office to rent the canoes while we wives were waiting in the back of the pickup. A bakery truck parked beside us. When the fellow went to the back of his truck to open the doors, the women yelled, "Cookie! Cookie! We want a cookie!" They sounded just like the Cookie Monster. They startled the fellow with their bellowing and they kept repeating, "Cookie." As he reached into his truck, he looked at us and smiled. Then he walked toward us and threw a couple boxes of cookies into the back of the pickup truck. He didn't say a word. I was a little embarrassed; however, I was the only one. They all laughed hysterically and proceeded to treat themselves to the cookies. They actually opened the packages and ate just like the Cookie Monster and repeated, "Cookie! Cookie!" as they munched away. Their behavior was a little peculiar. They couldn't wait to tell the fellows about the free cookies. The fellows came out of the office with grins on their faces. Before the girls could say anything, the economist in the group said, "Boy did we get a deal on these canoes." He told the fellow in the office that we were all laid off from work and could he give us a discount. The fellow was very convincing so the manager gave us a reduced rate. All of the guys were skilled tool and die machinists or other skilled workers and were making a comfortable living. I don't know what possessed them to do these things; maybe, the fresh mountain air was responsible. They jumped into the pickup and we followed a fellow in a truck loaded with our canoes. They took us upstream so we could canoe downstream. I guess canoeing downstream is easier.

When we arrived at the start of the trip the guys started unloading the canoes. I was shocked to see one of the fellows get into a canoe with a paddle in hand and slide down the rough dirt river bank into the water below. The rest of us waited for the workers to put the canoes into the water before we got into them. Tom and I were struggling with the canoe and paddles; we kept going around in circles. Then we changed positions, with him in the back and me in the front; it was a real challenge trying to change positions in a canoe in the river. He thought the distribution of weight would make a difference. I don't know, maybe it was how we paddled; anyway, we finally made it to the middle of the river. We slowly started drifting down the Clarion River with the current and our rowing skills. Then we noticed our friends canoeing straight toward us from all directions. They didn't say anything; they just kept coming closer and closer. As I looked at the face of one friend, I saw revenge in his eyes. Instantly, I thought back to grade school when I *accidently* threw his lunch into the slop ditch. The operative word here is *accidently*. Well, he deserved it! But what had I done to the rest of them. They were coming at us with a vengeance and looked possessed. I tried talking to them, but no one answered. They just kept rowing toward us. They circled our canoe and started poking and pushing it. Before long they tipped the canoe over. Splash! Into the water I went in my new outfit! They all laughed and cheered and continued down the river! No one stopped to help. Apparently, it's another tradition to tip over the canoe of the newcomers. I guess since the other new comers got soaked with a bucket of water the night before, they felt we should be dumped into the river. Thank goodness, the water was only waist high where they tipped us over. In my wildest dream, I never thought they would have dumped us into the river since these people were our longtime best friends.

After much struggling, we got our canoe turned over and managed to climb inside; we tried to paddle downstream. However, we lost our momentum and were going around in circles again. Finally, we got the canoe flowing downstream and were on our way. As we slowly inched our way downstream I looked around and didn't notice any smooth sailing canoes among the bunch. They looked like the Keystone Cops canoeing down the river. Since most of them do this every summer, I thought they would be skilled. But they weren't.

By the time we got back to our camp, everyone was soaking wet. I changed into another new outfit especially for this weekend and went to lunch. During lunch, the group decided to go horseback riding. I declined for two reasons. First, I am deathly afraid of horses, and second, I didn't want to endure anymore traditions. Tom and I stayed at the shack and recuperated from our wild, wet, physically exhausting canoe ride while the cowboys went horseback riding.

They were gone for a couple of hours, and we were finally able to rest. When they came back they had many stories to tell. A horse ran away with one of the fellows through the woods. Another horse followed the trails for a short time and then turned around and ran straight back into the stables. One horse wouldn't go at all. Apparently, the horses had minds of their own or just maybe these horses remembered this crew from other years and were displaying a little revenge.

The guys fixed another campfire and the gals fixed supper. Again, I sat on a log in a new outfit sipping on my chardonnay around a campfire. It's amazing the amount of fun you can have sitting around a campfire with lifelong friends. A couple fellows got enjoyment from pushing everyone's buttons. Just one statement could set someone off on a tangent. For instance, all you have to say is, "That's a true fact." And one gal starts chattering, "There is no such statement. If it's a fact, it's true. You don't have to say true fact. There is no such thing as a false fact. Then it wouldn't be a fact." She just went on and on like the Energizer Bunny. When she finally calmed down, someone would nonchalantly say "true fact" and she would start her chatter all over again. All night long, they were pushing people's buttons. Our friend tried to tell another joke, and there was a contest to see who would be the last man standing. Tom and I won this contest in spite of how tired we were. We weren't about to get a bucket of water poured over us.

The next day, we all were up bright and early with the birds. We ate breakfast and went hiking in the woods. After our hike, one of the guys announced, "It's time to play baseball!" A fellow got an oversized plastic bat and ball, and everyone proceeded across the road into a field. I reluctantly followed. It amazes me how grown men turn into little boys when they play a game and how competitive they are and extremely serious they become. They argue about whose on which team, which team is up first, whose turn it is, who is out, and who is safe. This behavior seemed a little strange to me since the range of players were from jocks who play on a team every summer to beer-belly couch potatoes who haven't picked up a bat in twenty years. The gals ranged from tomboys who play on a real team to long-nailed, pricy-fancy ladies who didn't know which end of the bat to hold, a pregnant lady and everything in between. The players also knew whose buttons to push during games and deliberately did things to get a response from others.

After the game, we went back to the shacks and the girls fixed dinner and the guys started packing the cars. After dinner, we straightened up the camping area and headed home. That is, everyone except Tom and me. After this adventure I was really looking forward to a day of complete rest without any unbearable traditions or escapades. This weekend with our friends was not what I had anticipated. I had no idea what adventures they endured. They led us to believe they stayed in comfy, cozy cabins, rested, hiked a little on the trails, and had a peaceful canoe ride down the Clarion River. Wow, was I deceived! It wasn't the weekend I had envisioned.

Tom and I checked into the motel and collapsed onto the bed, exhausted and grubby. Before long we fell asleep. Suddenly, we were awakened to a loud pounding on the door. We couldn't imagine who it would be. The pounding didn't cease so Tom got up and peaked out the window and it was a couple of our camping friends. Apparently, one of our friends got wind of our plan to go to a motel and they drove around to all the motels until they saw our car. I told Tom not to answer the door, but they were relentless. They made so much racket and pounded so hard that I was afraid they were going to break down the door. Tom opened the door and, much to my surprise, they handed Tom a bottle of wine and a couple of wineglasses. Of course, Tom being the romantic he is offered his buddies some wine. They declined. They stayed for a while and we talked about the highlights of the trip and then they left.

Now our romantic weekend had officially started. Tom put his arms around me and started to laugh. I asked, "What's so funny?" He answered, "I thought I was kissing you and I kissed my own arm." Oh! My romantic husband! This was a typical start for our romantic weekend. Anyway!

For sure, there would be absolutely nothing short of a death that would keep us from going to Cook Forest the next summer because I absolutely had to be on the other side of the "traditions."

The next summer, we worked out our schedule to free us for the Cook Forest trip. As we were driving through the forest to our destination, I didn't dream of a quiet, peaceful, and restful evening sipping chardonnay around a cozy fireplace while having quiet conversation with our lifelong friends. Maybe for the first time in my life, I knew exactly where I was going and what was going to happen. However, some unsuspecting friends of ours were driving this same road expecting a peaceful weekend with their "best" friends.

We arrived at our destination but the newcomers weren't there yet. So along with our friends we planned our strategies for the weekend. I noticed a restaurant was built right in the middle of our ball field but that didn't seem to bother anyone. It was exciting being on this end of the traditions.

When the newcomers arrived, I could see the disappointment on their faces as they looked around the camp area. They said something similar to what I said the year before. The same fellow said, "We like it better here so we can build a campfire. They built a restaurant in the middle of the field, but that won't bother us. We can still play ball." Again, a toss of the coin determined who was getting the pop-out couch, and, of course, it was the new couple.

Things paralleled the summer before, only I was prepared for the unexpected. The guys still didn't mature much since last year, and they still bickered about building the campfire. But in the end it was a magnificent campfire, and I sat on a log in my *old* camping clothes while sipping on my wine. Our friend still couldn't tell a joke, but he tried. And the same buttons were pushed with the same responses. It's amazing how predictable we all were.

Finally the new couple decided to go to bed, so we all told them good night and we would see them in the morning. The fellows waited until they got settled into bed, filled a bucket of water, quietly snuck into their bedroom, and poured it onto the unsuspecting couple. They high-tailed it out of the shack and innocently sat around the campfire and waited for the drenched couple to join us there. The same fellow greeted them with, "Back so soon?" He got a reply similar to the year before.

The next day we got up bright and early, ate breakfast, piled into the back of a pickup truck, and headed for the Clarion River to go canoeing. This is the day I waited for all year. Revenge is sweet, even though it's not the same people that toppled us. It was the unsuspecting newcomers. We got our canoes and headed upstream to enter the river. After everyone was in canoes, we waited until the prey has settled in and paddling down the river. The tension was mounting and then on cue we all headed toward the unsuspecting victims and surrounded them. They asked, "What are you doing?" No one answered. We were stoned faced and on signal we tipped over their canoe. Splat! Into the water they went. I felt a smug satisfaction as we nonchalantly continued rowing down the river.

We went back to the shacks and changed for dinner. We dined at the restaurant right smack in the middle of our ball field. The men looked out the window and planned their strategy for the next day's big game. I couldn't believe they would actually play ball with the restaurant smack dab in the middle of their field. However, the restaurant didn't seem to bother them.

After dinner the guys fixed a campfire and we sat around telling jokes, pushing buttons, and enjoying each other's company much the same as the nights before. While I was sitting enjoying the campfire I glanced over to the victims of this summer. I remembered the first time I met her. We were swimming at a park with the families of some of our mutual friends. I noticed her prancing around in a chocolate bikini like a model, and there wasn't a flaw on her body. I thought, "What is she doing here with all of us stretched-marked mothers?" Tom noticed her also! I said, "I bet she doesn't have any children." Later, I discovered she had four children. Then I said, "She probably has a messy house and can't cook." A few weeks later we were invited to her house. Her home was immaculate, the food was delicious, and her motherly interaction with her four children was very impressive. She was flawless, a perfect host, soft spoken, and made everyone feel at home. I couldn't help liking her. All I can say is God put people on this earth like her to make the rest of us feel bad. I couldn't believe how good she looked even after we drenched her with a bucket of water, dumped her into the river, and she just came back from horseback riding. She didn't have a hair out of place. I looked at the gals around me and we were grimy, to say the least. Apparently, I wasn't the only one thinking she was a little too well groomed for camping. One of the gals next to me said, "This isn't right. She looks too good. Come on let's mess her up a little." So we all got up and went over to her and someone said, "We are camping. You need to look like us." So we messed up her hair. She just laughed and shook her head and ran her fingers through her hair and, presto, she was a model again. We gave up and sat down. No one wanted to be the first to go to bed. I wonder why? So we all kind of went at the same time.

The next morning, after breakfast, a fellow picked up the oversized plastic bat and ball and said, "Let's go!" Like zombies we all followed. We played our game of ball as though the restaurant wasn't there. I expected someone to come out any minute and chase us away, but amazingly no one seemed to care or maybe we were their live entertainment for the day. This surely was a silly sight—eight slightly overweight, balding, middle aged men playing ball with an oversized plastic bat and bickering over every little thing. The wives just waited and went where the men told us to go. After the game, we packed and headed home. It's hard to believe that I participated in some of these antics. It must have been that fresh mountain air.

The cartoon character planned the family vacations and they always centered on him. At first he planned short day trips to the Air Force museum, Gettysburg, air shows, and long drives in the mountains. Every fall, Tom insisted on driving the family through the mountains to see the colorful leaves on the trees. The children didn't appreciate his trips. After we were on the road for a while they all fell asleep; they weren't eager to get to his destination. This was the start of their resistance and complaining when we went on trips.

As the children grew older, the family vacations didn't get better. One of the organizations Tom belongs to was hosting an annual oyster bake; he wanted us to go with him. I told Tom, "There are two problems: it was halfway across the state and I don't like oysters and neither do the children. Why do you want us to go?" With some of his reassuring logic he said, "It will be a nice educational drive for the children and they will have other things to eat at the oyster bake." Reluctantly, I agreed to go on the trip. Tom called and made our reservations.

I don't know how educational the trip across the state was since they all fell asleep. When we arrived we noticed it was an outside picnic, which was fine because it was a beautiful day. We skipped lunch so everyone was hungry. Tom went to the gate and paid for our tickets, and we proceeded to the picnic area. I felt like I was in oyster land. The first thing I saw was a tent with men constantly shucking oysters. The pile was taller than any human. The smell was nauseating if you didn't like oysters. Then my eyes noticed a group of people gathered around a large table sucking the raw oysters out of the shell! "Yuck!" There was a large steamer with steamed oysters, a large tub with ice filled with raw oysters, a big pot over a fire filled with oyster soup, a fryer filled with deep fried oysters, and an oven filled with baked oysters. Oysters were everywhere. Anyway you could think of fixing an oyster, they did it. They even had oyster crackers for the oyster soup.

Tom appeared to be in oyster heaven as he walked around like a kid in a candy store devouring every type of oyster along the way while we walked gagging as we went. At one point I tried an oyster out of sheer hunger gagged and spit it out. I didn't even feel the slightest embarrassment since everyone around me was slurping, sucking, chucking, and licking their fingers. Lora discovered she liked oysters. So she and Tom walked around devouring oysters while the rest of us found a shady place to sit. We pondered where to go to eat after we left this oyster pit. Of course, Tom wanted to make a day of it and socialize with the fellows he knew from the organizations.

Tom looks back at that event thinking we all had the best day ever. Maureen, Marty, and I look back on this day as a complete nightmare! There was not one morsel of any other food. Oyster bake they said, and an oyster bake it was.

Tom planned a relaxing weekend away from the children and the stress of everyday living; however, as usual, it wasn't very relaxing. We went to a convention of an organization he belonged to, and while Tom was at meetings I went sight-seeing with some of the wives. We waited outside the hotel for our tour guide. A broken down contraption pulled up in front of us. We reluctantly went into the machine and toured the town. While touring, we started jerking from the driver pumping the brakes. We landed in the center of a busy intersection before we got stopped. Either the driver wasn't paying attention or the breaks weren't working properly. Either way, an officer stopped to talk to the driver and gave him a warning to be careful. Then he proceeded down the highway and drove off the road, over a cliff, and into the water. We all screamed and were in a panic until some of the passengers calmed us down by explaining the contraption we were in could also float. Immediately we checked our brochure and it said, "Scenic Duck Tour." I guess the word "Duck" should have given us a clue to where this tour was going. But it didn't. I still felt uneasy because most of the contraption was immersed in water and I felt like we were sinking. I noticed people along the shore waving and trying to get our attention. We thought they were tourist and waved back. We floated on the river for a little while then he drove up a steep bank and back onto the road. He drove us back to our hotel. Later we discovered they were having problems with the "Duck" we were on. They weren't safe and many of them sunk. It didn't do too well on the road, either.

The next summer, Tom and I planned a trip to the Finger Lakes in New York for our little weekend getaway to relax without the children. Tom was excited about the trip, saying, "I always wanted to go there. It's nice and peaceful and not too far away."

The first thing we did when we arrived was go on a boat tour to learn the history of the Finger Lakes. The next day we drove to a Glen where water roared down the mountain. We climbed a massive amount of steps to the top. While climbing, we occasionally stopped and wandered off the path. In certain areas people walked across the Glen and sat on the cliffs. Some of the places we went I didn't feel too safe, but Tom said with some of his adventure logic, "If it was dangerous it would be roped off and they wouldn't let us walk around here." A couple of times we slipped on the rocks. There were many small pools of water where people were wading.

We were really tired after that hike up and down the Glen so we went back to our motel and rested. Later we went to dinner and then to the lounge for a glass of wine before retiring for the night. While I was sipping on my wine, the local news caught my attention, "A tourist drowned in the Glen earlier in the day." It was in the exact area where Tom and I were hiking earlier. Everyone in the lounge was shocked. The bartender informed us, "The Glen is very dangerous with the steep, slippery cliffs and the deep water in some areas. Every summer at least three tourists drown." I relived our day and was terrified of what could have happened to us if we would have lost our footing on the slippery rocks. After a while we regained our senses and started to relax again. Then a woman at the bar started choking and was grasping for her breath. Her loving husband was sitting beside her. He just sat there sipping his beer. Everyone was looking her way, concerned. Someone shouted, "Your wife is choking! Help her!" The husband answered, "Oh, it is just ice. It will melt before she dies." He sat unconcerned and continued drinking his beer. Our relaxing vacation ended with a little drama.

For some reason we are drawn to Erie, even though the first time we stayed in this town it was a total disaster. Tom neglected to make reservations for our wedding night and the only place that had rooms was a broken down hotel with prostitutes prancing around. (Refer to chapter two in *Help I Married a Cartoon Character*) I swore I would never stay in this town again.

Tom attends conferences in Erie every year and stays at a nice motel and eats at great seafood restaurants. One year, he asked me to go with him. I was reluctant to go, since the horrible experience on our wedding night forty-nine years ago haunts me. However, he said, "I will make reservations for a pool-side room at this great motel where you can sit on the balcony and write while I am at the meetings. Then we will go to dinner at a seafood restaurant overlooking the lake and watch the sunset." It sounded too good to pass up, so I agreed to go with him. We arrived at our motel in Erie and I went to the balcony and I couldn't believe my eyes: it was all boarded up. It was a small, enclosed, claustrophobic room and you couldn't see the pool. Apparently, the decorations for the pool were on the other side of this balcony. I told Tom the room was fine. I would walk down to the pool area later and write. When I went to the pool, I noticed dolphins painted on our boarded up balcony. After his meetings, we dressed up and went out to dinner. There was a slight problem: all the seafood restaurants he referred to were closed and boarded up. We drove around town looking for a good seafood restaurant but couldn't find one. I guess we weren't meant to have a good time in this town.

I think, subconsciously, I was determined to enjoy this town since the next year I went with Tom to Erie again on the condition he made sure to reserve a pool-side room that wasn't boarded up. This trip didn't have any surprises. I sat on my balcony and wrote while enjoying the calm scenic pool area. We found a couple fine seafood restaurants, and the cuisine was succulent. So over the past few years, we have gone to Erie a couple times a year to relax. Lake

Erie is located a couple miles down the street from our motel, so we occasionally drive to the beach. I would write and Tom would play with his gadgets while enjoying the sounds of roaring waves.

The last time we were there for the weekend, I wrote a couple chapters of my second book at the pool. Later we went to the lounge and I jotted some ideas for my book on a napkin. Someone noticed and asked, "What are you writing?" I told him about my books. A lady overheard and asked what my book was about. I told her some of the humorous stories. Then she started telling us funny stories about her life. Then she asked, "Can I be in your next book?" The story I liked the best was the time she got into an argument with her husband and she put a club on his sports car so he couldn't drive it. Then he put another club on the car so she couldn't drive it, either. So there sat the sports car in the garage. I guess, Tom and I aren't the only looney ones in this world.

We also got to know some people from Erie and asked them if they knew about the hotel where we spent our honeymoon night. They remembered and informed us it has been torn down for quite a while. They couldn't believe we actually spent our wedding night there. I can't believe it, either. Of course, Tom had no problem with the hotel of gruesomeness

The words rest, relaxation, and pleasure trip are used in the dictionary to describe a vacation. However, the words stress, anxiety, tension, and exhaustion describe our vacations. Many times Tom has to take off work a couple days after our vacations to rest.

9

Two Old Cartoon Characters
In Their Golden Years

Tom refers to our old age as the golden years; hence, we have already passed through our copper, nickel, and silver years. My copper years were full of great expectations; I believed everything I read or heard. I enjoyed life to the fullest; everything was beautiful and exciting. I looked forward to the changing of the seasons because each season was unique and magical. I loved scuffling through the waving grasses while sniffing the fragrance of the roses in spring. I danced around the beautiful yellow flowers that bloomed throughout the green grass. After a while they turned into white cotton balls and I picked them and blew on them until they flew into the wind. This was the season the Easter Bunny hopped down the bunny trail and delivered baskets full of candy. The payday before Easter, Mom took me shopping and bought me an Easter bonnet, spring coat, dress, and new shoes. I colored eggs on Easter Eve, went to bed early, and dreamed about the Easter bunny hopping down the bunny trail to my town.

In the summer when I got hungry, I would snack on fresh juicy strawberries, tomatoes, and cucumbers from the garden. We played baseball in the field across the street, and at night we played hide-n-seek. On really hot days we would pack a picnic basket and go to the river to swim.

In the fall I would skip through the multicolored leaves and when I came upon a pile I would leap into them and scatter the colorful leaves into the air. I would dress up on Halloween and go "trick or treating" with my friends. Afterward we would line up our candy and devour it a piece at a time.

The winters were magical with the sparkling snow all over the countryside. I rode my sled a quarter of a mile on the icy roads with my neighborhood friends. Dad would make homemade ice cream with the icicles I knocked down from the roof. We hiked into the woods and cut down a Christmas tree and put it in the corner of the living room. Then I eagerly waited for Christmas Eve when Santa came and decorated the tree and put a pile of presents under it just for me.

I was so excited when I lost my first tooth. I put it under my pillow and dreamed about the tooth fairy coming in the night, taking my tooth, and leaving me a quarter. With that quarter I walked to the Saturday matinee with my brother and bought my movie ticket, a candy bar, and had enough money left over for an ice cream soda at the drug store on the way home. I enjoyed going to the movie theater where all my favorite actors gathered to perform for me.

Every Saturday night we would go to my grandparents and watch wrestling. The wrestlers reminded me somewhat of how my brother and I acted on occasion. I enjoyed the sport and became a fan of some of the wrestlers. I marveled at their muscles and the extraordinary way they maneuvered themselves out of the hold of their opponents. It was exciting to watch the countdown when someone was pinned to the mat. I would count along with the referee when a fellow was pinned; however, if one of my favorites was pinned to the mat I would watch hoping he would yank an extra surge of strength from his body and jump up and throw his opponent across the ring. It was suspenseful.

Washington, D.C., looked so impressive on television, especially in the spring when the cherry blossoms were in bloom. The White House appeared like a huge estate with acres and acres of land. I looked forward to one day going to the White House and roaming around the cherry blossoms and absorbing the history of our country.

I marveled at the Niagara Falls because at the time some considered it one of the Seven Wonders of the World and it was often referred to as the honeymoon capital of the world. I envisioned this gigantic mountain (somewhat like the Andes) with violent roaring water rushing down the mountain surrounded by an enchanting land where you could roam. I often dreamed of meeting my Prince Charming and having a beautiful wedding and elegant reception. Then he would scoop me up into his arms and take me to Niagara Falls. There just couldn't be a more romantic place to go than the honeymoon capital of the world. We would walk through the enchanted land holding hands while watching the breathtaking falls from a distance. Afterward, we would live happily ever after just like the princesses in my story books.

My nickel years were a harsh reality enlightenment and full of disappointment. I no longer believed everything I heard or read. I no longer looked forward to the changing of the seasons because everything I loved about them was destroyed as I grew older. The beautiful yellow flowers that I used to dance through were considered a menace and were sprayed with poison and never again turned into the cotton balls I blew into the wind. I discovered there wasn't an Easter Bunny, and that realization took all the joy out of coloring the eggs and my basket full of candy was replaced with a hollow chocolate bunny. My new clothes hung in the closet for special occasions, and I always grew out of them before anything special happened. Then Mom gave them to my cousin who wore them whenever she wanted.

In the summer I had to start weeding the garden and picking strawberries, tomatoes, and cucumbers for Mom to make jelly, sauce, and pickles. I had to wash jars and help with the canning. A house was built in the field where we played baseball. I could no longer go to the river to swim because a closed sign was posted at the area.

In the fall Dad handed me a rake and I had to gather hundreds and hundreds of leaves into a pile so he could burn them. I was too old to go "trick or treating" on Halloween and didn't get any more candy to line up and devour.

In the winter Dad handed me a shovel and I had to remove the snow off the sidewalk and driveway. The country roads were salted and that ended my sled ridding. Dad put me in charge of cranking the ice cream freezer, and it was no longer fun gathering the ice from the eves. We went to the corner gas station and bought our Christmas tree since it was easier than hiking through the woods and chopping one down. All the joy of the Christmas season was gone when I discovered there wasn't a Santa Claus.

I also discovered there wasn't a tooth fairy and that was the end of my quarters. However, it didn't matter much since my teeth stopped falling out. I learned my favorite actors weren't at the theater to perform for me; instead, there was a machine with film in a small room in the back of the theater.

I went to a real wrestling match in Pittsburgh with some friends. I couldn't believe my eyes. There were posters of people for an audience, and the wrestling didn't look like it was portrayed on television. They just flopped and danced around. The holds from our angle were truly only acting. Every so often a lady who was not even watching the match would go in front of the camera and shake a rubber chicken and yell. Then she would sit down for a while and get up and shake the chicken again. When we left I couldn't stop talking about my disappointment and how different it was portrayed on television. Wrestling was a hoax. I was deceived.

Three of my friends and I decided to go to Washington, D.C., for the Cherry Blossom Festival. Again I was totally disappointed when I viewed the White House. At first I didn't think it was the White House since it looked so small compared to my great expectations. A few estates in Sharpsville were just as impressive. Now, I'm by no means talking about the history and the interior of the White House; the tour was quite memorable and moving. The outside as I viewed on television looked much larger and the property appeared like acres and acres. I wasn't especially impressed with the cherry blossoms since they seemed no different than the beautiful blossoms that bloom every spring at the park a short distance from where I live.

For years I planned to go to Niagara Falls on my honeymoon even before I met my Prince Charming. When the big day finally arrived, Prince Charming and I traveled to the falls; I was overwhelmed with disappointment. For years I had anticipated this gigantic mountain (somewhat like the Andes) with violent roaring water rushing down the mountain. Well it was more like rushing water over a hillside compared to my great expectations. Other than seeing many people walking around holding hands and looking starry-eyed at each other, I couldn't find anything significant for honeymooners. Now, I'm not even going to talk about meeting my Prince Charming, marriage, and living happily ever after. All I have to say is, I had great expectations!

My silver years were my busiest since I acquired many more roles and found them overlapping. The demands of each were overwhelming. The role of a wife was difficult since this is when I realized my Prince Charming was a cartoon character and lived by logic he made up as he journeyed through life. The most rewarding and demanding role was a mother.

This was a time when we traveled twenty miles to a hot dog shop for the best chilidogs around. The cook was a legend who entertained us while we were waiting for our hotdogs. He would line up buns on his sweaty, hairy arm, and then quickly place a hotdog into each bun. He expertly squirted mustard, spooned onions, and spurt chili sauce on them. Then he turned his arm and, zoom, the hotdogs landed in white paper holders. He added a few fries and, presto, lunch was served. We would devour our hotdogs while watching him prepare another batch. Tom was proud of the fact he could eat six chilidogs for lunch.

Every so often we risked our lives and traveled to a tavern in a rundown section of a town ten miles away for the best steak dinner in the world. Weeds and dirt were everywhere. The tavern was so dirty on the outside you couldn't see through the windows. The inside was filthy, and we wouldn't use the restrooms. But the steak was so tender you could cut it with your fork. I don't particularly care for steak; however, this one was juicy, succulent, and to die for. The risk was well worth it.

I have traveled along the East Coast from the tip of Maine to the tip of Florida and as far west as Texas. I have seen the wonders in twenty-five states. However, I haven't seen any place in all those states where I would want to live more than Sharpsville. What I enjoy most is the visit from Santa Claus. He visits every house in Sharpsville at Christmas. I lived here since I was three-years old and have everything I need within a three mile radius. I enjoy a beautiful park and a free golf course. Penn State Shenango University is five minutes away. I attended many classes there, and now that I am in my golden years I can attend classes for a small activity fee.

Shenango dam and a picnic area are nearby where we spend many afternoons. There are several churches of different denominations. We wine and dine at a variety of restaurants. Talented people from all over perform in our Opera house. Two floral shops flourish even though Tom has never stepped foot in them.

In our golden years, we are often referred to as senior citizens, and Tom detests being called one. One advantage is numerous restaurants offer you a discount on meals; I don't hesitate to take advantage of the discounts. Tom, on the other hand, is very adamant about not revealing his age and would rather pay full price than disclose he is a senior citizen. One day, he went to a restaurant for a take-out order. This particular restaurant gave senior discounts, so I told him to make sure he got it. He said, "I'm not telling anyone I'm a senior citizen." Later, I glanced at the receipt from the restaurant and said, "Well, I'm glad you finally took advantage of the discount." He asked, "What are you talking about?" I showed him the receipt and in large letters the words "Senior Discount." Surprised, he stated, "I didn't tell anyone I was a senior citizen." I laughed and said, "They just took a look at you and gave you the discount! That's worse than telling them." He was speechless, and for once I wasn't zapped with his logic; he just gave me a pathetic look.

Tom surely acts like someone in his senior years, such as the time we were traveling and stopped for a pizza. I wasn't sure how to order since it looked like a restaurant, but it had a counter that appeared like a take-out place. While I was debating whether to sit at a table or go to the counter and order, Tom said, "Go up and order. I will get a table." I asked, "What do you want?" Annoyed, he answered, "The usual. You know I always get pepperoni pizza. I have been getting the same pizza for years." Before I got to the counter, a waitress came from the back room and said, "I'll take your order at the table." So I sat down, and when the waitress came over for our order much to my surprise Tom ordered a pizza with pineapple and ham. Never in his life had he eaten a pizza with pineapple and ham. I wondered, "How could he be so adamant about me ordering him a pepperoni pizza a few minutes ago, but then he picks a pineapple-ham pizza." You would think there wouldn't be any surprises in our golden years.

We have come a long way since our honeymoon when we were at an elegant restaurant at Niagara Falls and pondered if we should eat our pasta out of the bowl it was served in or pour the pasta onto the plate that was beneath the bowl. We felt self conscious and whispered to each other trying to figure out the proper etiquette. We fretted about our decision to pour the spaghetti from the bowl onto the plate in case it was the wrong thing to do. These days, we just do what we want and don't fret about what people think.

We still check our old-age poster that reveals how and when the body deteriorates from time to time to see what part will deteriorate next. I am sad to say Tom and I are right on the calculated expectation, and I guess knowing is half the battle. Likewise, there was a time when I got into the car on a hot summer day and I would cringe from the hot seats, but now I find the hot car seat soothing to my aching body.

Recently, I went to a new doctor for my annual physical and the nurse measured my height and said, "You are 5'4"." I answered, "No! I am 5'6"." She measured me again and said, "No, you are 5'4"." I replied, "That's impossible! I have been 5'6" since I was fourteen years old!" She measured me again and persisted, "You are 5'4" I have to put that height on your chart." I got my purse and insisted, "Check my driver license!" She appeared a little annoyed, so I put my purse back and said no more but thought, "I am 5'6" and the first thing I am going to do when I get home is measure myself. I am *not* shrinking!"

Some doctors really have poor bedside manners. I went to my gynecologist and he wanted me to take some medicine that had side effects. When I questioned him about them, I must have perturbed him a little (imagine that) because he said, "You are not going to live forever. You are going to die from something. What do you want to die from? Blood clots, heart disease, or cancer? What do you want it to be?" I answered, "What about old age?" He insisted I take the medicine, so I reluctantly took the prescription and left his office. I didn't fill the prescription, and after much thought I chose another gynecologist who didn't feel the medication was necessary. So here I am: old and still alive twenty-two years later.

One day, I moved a certain way and it felt as though something shifted inside my body. When I went to the doctor for my yearly checkup, he asked, "Are you having any problems?" I said, "I moved a certain way and it feels like something shifted in my body." I pointed to the area, and after he examined it, he replied, "Oh, that is just a piece of fat." I don't think so!!! If that were the case there would be a great deal of shifting going on in there!

I have noticed an unexpected problem arises in one's golden years. Children in your neighborhood grow up and become your car salesmen, doctors, dentists, and nurses. The last time I went to the eye doctor, a girl from the neighborhood came in to examine my eyes. I cringed when I went to the doctor's office and another neighborhood girl took my vitals. When I went to the hospital, a fellow from the neighborhood took my information. I immediately thought of our relationship when "these kids" were growing up. I was very pleased because they were very knowledgeable and professional. Yet, when I saw an old paperboy working as a salesman at the local car dealer, I just drove on by.

One factor, I didn't consider in my golden years was the cartoon character would be retired and home all day and night. I didn't realize he would invade my space and always be in my way. Everywhere I went, the kitchen, bathroom, patio, bedroom, living room and even outside, there he was. I couldn't escape him. He was always giving his illogical opinion about my cooking, cleaning and shopping. He even feels the arrangements of the things inside my cupboards are all wrong. I have been doing these things for over fifty years, and I would like to think I have mastered the simple things of life, such as arranging cupboards, cleaning and cooking. He reminds me of someone hired fresh from college who is book smart but lacks experience. As if I'm going to listen to someone who has never washed a dish, arranged a cupboard, cooked a meal, cleaned a house or washed laundry. He talks the talk, but he doesn't walk the walk. Over the years, by trial and error, I ran an efficient household, so now I can sit back and relax since I am organized and know where everything is at a moment's notice. I don't need Mr. High-Tech to advise me. I told him, "You are welcome to arrange the cupboards, do the shopping, cooking, and cleaning. I will gladly step aside and change roles with you. I am sure I can sit with my feet propped up and read a book while you serve me." This shut him up for a while. No high-tech nerd is going to tell me how to run the household as they sip on their Starbuck's coffee.

Last summer, we decided to remodel the kitchen and living room. When it came to choosing paint I never thought in a million years that I would be someone who pondered over which shade of white to use for my kitchen and living room. A few years ago, I discovered white paint was mixed at the hardware store and there were over fifty shades. Again, all I wanted was the white paint called off white back in the day. Nevertheless, here I sat pondering. I was forced into this dilemma since they don't make off white anymore. I finally found two colors that appeared off white. I chose Artist's Canvas for the kitchen and Cream in my Coffee for the living room. Little did I realize this would be the least of my pondering.

Tom decided to tear up the old tile and install a new one in the kitchen to save money. After he tore up the old tile, he discovered many rough spots that needed sanded so he headed off to the hardware store and purchased two sanders, knee pads, a roller, brush, and glue for a total of more than $400, and he hadn't even bought the tile yet. He stated, "Save money." Really! This was more than it would have cost to purchase the tile and have it installed. I always get the urge to whack him upside the head when he comes home from the high-tech store, but I never thought in a million years I would get that urge when he came home from the hardware store. Wonders never cease.

He didn't sand the floor all at once; he sanded it a little and stopped. I would clean up the kitchen and then he would sand a little more. This went on for a while until I went into my crazy lady act and demanded he finish with the sanding!

Tom takes such pride in the fact that he is 100% Irish and is always referring to it. He is impossible and obnoxious on St. Patrick's Day. He spends the day at a local tavern drinking green beer dressed like his version of a leprechaun along with his Irish buddies and the want-to-be Irish for the day. He calls himself a thoroughbred and me a Mongrel since I am a mixture of a few nationalities. He considers himself superior to me; however, he continually proves himself wrong. For instance, one time he moved the refrigerator out so he could work on the back wall before the painter came. He kept tripping on the cord when he went to get a tool or whatever. The

Mongrel was enjoying the Irishman's problem. However, she didn't want the cord to be pulled out of the back of the fridge when he tripped so she pushed the refrigerator over a little so the Irishman wouldn't trip and could still get to the back wall.

Can you just picture the comic strip or hear the joke? How many times does an Irishman trip over a cord to the refrigerator that he moved out so he could fix the back wall? Once, "Wow!! I almost killed myself." Twice, "What the heck?" Third time, "Holy cow!" Fourth time, "How in the world, I almost fell." Now the Mongrel moves the refrigerator a little and solves the Irishman's problem. Tell me again who is superior!

Living in the same small town for sixty-seven years and having ancestors who settled here a hundred years ago and married to someone whose ancestors settled here, it's hard to go anywhere where someone doesn't know me. The restaurants in town are owned by neighbors and fellow classmates. The president of a bank in town is a classmate of mine. The grocery stores, hospital, and mall are full of employees that are relatives or friends, and now some of our friends have retired and their children are taking over. Every time I go grocery shopping, I run into a friend; it's not unusual to spend an hour visiting. We must catch up on the latest in our lives; never mind, the ice cream is melting, the milk souring, and the lettuce wilting. Sometimes I find myself hiding from a friend if I am in a hurry. There are a couple friends, if we bump into each other; it is an hour of conversation, guaranteed. We just can't help it.

One afternoon, my daughter and I went shopping. The hostess of the restaurant we chose for lunch seated us near a golf buddy of Tom's and his wife, a couple whom we had known forever. Later, we went to the book store and I ran into a girl I used to babysit. While I was talking to the lady at the register, another person from my neighborhood, I felt a tap on my shoulder. The person said, "I just knew that was you; I heard this voice and just had to check and see if it was you." This fellow I knew since first grade. Lora also ran into some of her friends at the mall. Next we went to the grocery store and ran into my priest; I immediately morphed into my holy mode. The cashier was my friend; I used to babysit her children. Another cashier was the daughter of my daughter's friend. Visiting with all these people and shopping for three hours was exhausting.

I am surrounded by people who know everything about me and my descendants. In my golden years, I have reached a point where I want to go where nobody knows my name. I want to talk to people who don't know everything about me and my family. I am looking for fresh conversation with people who don't know what I am going to say, and finish my sentences. I knew that would be impossible in this town; therefore, I joined a book club at a church in the next town. The first day of the book club I left the house full of anticipation of finally talking to people who didn't already know me, of me, or my family, or Tom, or Tom's family. I entered the room and there were twenty ladies seated around a table. At first glance, I didn't recognize anyone and felt a calm relief. I sat down and started talking to some of the ladies before the discussion about the book started. Upon closer look, I couldn't believe my eyes. My eighth grade school teacher was there, and when we introduced ourselves, three people knew my husband's family. But worst of all, the head of the book club had just been to some meetings that Tom attended and they butted heads on a few issues. My fresh conservation was ended before it started. What was I thinking? Tom's parents' family lived in the area for a hundred years, as did my parent's family. I guess I will have to go the next state.

Nevertheless, I joined another book club in another town. I thought about using my maiden name, but after much thought I realized that just as many people would know my relatives as they do Tom's. Then I pondered about using my mom's maiden name. However, much to my delight I didn't recognize anyone at the book club, and when they introduced themselves they only used their first names. I was so happy no one inquired about who I was or where I came from. We just lived for the moment and discussed the present and the book for the evening. It was a great two hours.

Maureen was in town for a couple of weeks the next time book club met. I invited her to go with me to meet the great bunch of ladies. She was reluctant about going since she had a full day and just wanted to relax. However, when I was getting ready to leave she changed her mind and off we went. When we got to the coffee shop where the book club meets, I went up and ordered a smoothie.

While they were making it, I looked around and the owner was running a sweeper and I noticed some of the lights were out. I asked where the ladies for the book club were, and he answered, "They just left." I said, "What! Book club is tonight at 7:00-9:00." He informed me, "No it's from 5:00-7:00, and I will be closing in a few minutes." Then Maureen grabbed the bookmark with the time and date and headed toward the manager to scold him, "Why would you have it 7-9 on the book marker?" As she said this she took a better look at the time on the bookmark and backed off. It clearly stated, "Book Club 5-7 on the fourth Wednesday of the month." She apologized and gave me some non-verbal language. I just said, "Oops." As I headed toward Maureen with my smoothie, she scolded, "Mother!" We burst out laughing. I replied, "I'm not going home! I am going to discuss this book. Let's go to for a wine and I will tell you about the book." Later Maureen asked, "How could you go at the wrong time? It's right on bookmark; didn't you look?" At some point in my golden years, our roles got reversed and I find myself getting scolded more and more by my children. I can't get used to the reversed roles so I always answer, "Oops!"

I always drank out of canning jars when I was growing up, and recently I started using them again because I have broken so many glasses over the years and am tired of replacing them every couple of months. Tom complains about them; however, I reminded him of a time when a little restaurant in Mercer served drinks in canning pint jars and he thought it was so cool. After a while, he discovered the canning jar glasses with a handle in a store so he bought a couple. I reminded him of his purchase and his use of the glasses. He said with some of his jar logic, "That was then and now is now." One night after he complained about the canning jars in the cupboard, we started watching his favorite show. The main character and another fellow were in a scene in which they drank out of the same jars I have in my cupboard. Now that's perfect timing.

Currently, they are making long-stemmed wine glasses from canning jars. Friends of ours were at a local tavern and they brought their daughter a canning jar wine glass for a birthday gift. I asked where they purchased the wine glass because I just had to have one.

Another reminder that I am in my golden years came when I took my towels from the line and carried them into the patio to fold. I picked up a hand towel from the basket and I hadn't a clue of how to fold it. I held it in my hands for a while just looking at it. I had been folding towels in the same manner for over forty years, and now all of a sudden I cannot remember how to fold this hand towel. I fold the towels a certain way so they will fit neatly into the closet. I couldn't remember if I folded it in half then in half again then over, or if I folded it in half then long way in half then over. So I got up and went into the bathroom closet and checked to see how the towels were folded. Then I proceeded to fold my towels. This problem-solving method will work as long as I don't use all of the towels in the closet.

I journeyed through my copper, nickel, and silver years and one thing I noticed is that women are expected to give and give and give. My roles are less now, and we are living our golden years to the fullest. We usually get where we are going in spite of a couple of false starts, getting to places on the wrong days, early, or late. Regardless of all of the aches and pains, we still manage to keep busy with our hobbies and interests. My gardening hasn't improved over the years. This fall Tom went into the living room and shouted, "Your artificial plant is shedding its leaves." I went to see what he was talking about and on the floor were leaves from my artificial plant. My baking hasn't improved either, and Tom has noticed. But I don't think this comment was appropriate, "Are you baking something?" No, I replied. He stated, "Oh, it must be a skunk." The highlight of my golden years so far was when a young gentleman called me a "Cougar." The golden years are a magnificent time of our lives.

10

Where The Cartoon
Characters Are Now

Now that we are in our golden years you might think we would sit back and relax; however, we are busier than ever. Tom's old boss called and asked him to teach a few skilled trades classes a week; apparently, there is a shortage of skilled trade tool and die workers and machinists. Employers are imploring men to enter the skilled training classes and begging men to come out of retirement to meet the demand. This seems bizarre since a few years earlier employers were offering skilled trades employees thousands of dollars to retire early. I just don't get it. Tom refused to go back to work full-time; however, he enjoys teaching classes six to eight hours a week. He is still a volunteer fireman and spends time at the station a couple days a week.

Tom is still fascinated with the latest technology and has a gadget for everything. The other day, he said he was going to spray the weeds in the cracks of the driveway. He has a contraption that fits over his shoulder with a hose attached to zap the weeds with poison. Since I don't like poison sprayed around and there weren't that many weeds in the cracks, I told Tom, "I will pull the weeds." He replied with some of his gadget logic, "It's better to poison them than pull them." I put on my garden gloves and started pulling the weeds while he was loading his contraption with poison and strapping it over his shoulder. By the time he came out of the garage to zap the weeds, the low-tech method had the job done. He looked like one of the ghost busters standing there all equipped to destroy the invaders.

Tom continues to refer to himself as a caring romantic; a few days before Valentine's Day, Tom announced, "I'll make the supreme sacrifice and spend the day with you on Valentine's Day. We will start off the day at our favorite coffee shop. Then I'll take you to the movies and then to our favorite tavern for a pizza." I thought, "What is this? Is he finally realizing what the word romantic means?" I should have been suspicious, but again my heart got in the way of common sense. On Valentine's Day, we headed for the coffee shop and enjoyed our brew and a bagel. Then we headed down the street to the movies. On the way to the movies I saw a sign in front of a floral shop that read, "A Dozen Roses $19.99." I thought, "What type of women get a dozen roses for Valentine's Day? Certainly not me! What type of man buys their woman roses for Valentine's Day; certainly not my man!"

The movie was hilarious; we laughed out loud and thoroughly enjoyed ourselves. After the movie he took me to our favorite tavern where the waiter gave me a red carnation and wished me a happy Valentine's Day. We ordered our pizza and a friend bought us a round of drinks. After a while another friend came over and said to Tom, "Can I buy you a drink? I left the house a couple of hours ago with this $20.00 bill and I haven't spent it yet. Every time my glass gets low, someone buys me a drink." Tom said, "I know what you mean. I started the day at the coffee shop and got a free bagel. Then I took my wife to the movies and we got in free. They have a policy at the Cinema that firemen and their guest get in free. Monday is free popcorn day and today is Monday. They just gave my wife a red carnation. I ordered a pizza and today it's on special for $5.00. As soon as I sat down my buddy over there bought Liz and me a drink. I ordered another drink and it was happy hour. I put a dollar in the lotto machine and won fifteen dollars." Wow! Again he deleted the romance from our day. I wonder why he is frugal when it comes to me and is such a spendthrift when it comes to his gadgets. And just why is he so happy and bragging about the fact he took his wife out for Valentine's Day for practically nothing. My frugal side agreed with him, but somehow I got this uneasy feeling that something was missing. Especially since Tom doesn't have a frugal side. I couldn't quite put my finger on it. Tom just seemed a little too pleased about taking me out on Valentine's Day for practically nothing.

I have survived years of "Lally Logic" by kicking into "Liz's Revenge" when the going got rough. I usually don't get angry when Tom zaps me with his unreasonable logic; however, I do get even. A couple things come to mind. He insisted on purchasing expensive envelopes at his high-tech store. I told him the same envelopes are five dollars cheaper at the low-tech store down the street. He said, "Those aren't any good. These ones are better." I couldn't see any difference between the two envelopes except the price. So I simply went to the discount store and purchased the same type of envelopes. Then I went to his desk and switched the expensive envelopes with the cheaper ones. He doesn't know the difference. Periodically, I put cheap envelopes into his expensive envelope box so he won't run out. He never has noticed that he hasn't run out of envelopes in two years. I also did this with his u-post-it notes.

My favorite "Liz's Revenge" was when I was in my daycare looking out the window and noticed Tom pulling into the driveway. I got my car keys and waited until he got out of the car, then I popped the trunk open. He stopped and closed the trunk and turned to walk away. I popped the trunk opened again. He turned toward the car and closed the trunk again. When he walked away, I popped the trunk again. He turned and while he was closing the trunk I started the car. I decided to stop before he caught on so I could do this *revenge* another day. All the while I watched him talking to himself, and his reaction was hilarious.

Sometimes I think Tom's logic may be rubbing off on me when it comes to my cleaning. I made up a poem that describes my feelings lately toward cleaning: I used to do an extensive cleaning in the spring and fall. Now, I just clean in the fall. Pretty soon, I won't clean at all.

I still don't share my fried green tomatoes and potato pancakes. I am like the story-book character who asked for help growing her wheat, making the flour, and baking the bread. None of her friends would help; however, when the bread was baked everyone wanted a slice. But she wouldn't share. My daughter often tells of the time I wouldn't share my potato pancakes with her. Potato pancakes take a lot of preparation, so I asked her to help me peel and grate the potatoes. However, she had more important things to do. I spent an hour peeling, washing, and grating the potatoes and onions and skinned my knuckles on the grater. Next I mixed flour and egg into the grated potatoes. Finally, they were ready to fry. I fried the first batch in my iron skillet and when it was a golden brown, Lora got a plate and was about to help herself when I pulled the potato pancakes away from her and said, "I'm "Henny Penny." However, I let her have some of the next batch but the first batch was for "Henny Penny" to devour.

In the spring, I travel to the local nursery and pick out the best tomato plants. I bring them home, transplant, fertilize, feed, water and talk to them. I watch them grow and when the green tomatoes are the precise size, I wash, slice, and fry them in an iron skillet. When they are a golden brown, everyone comes out of the woodwork wanting to devour my fried green tomatoes. My daughter actually told her daughter who wasn't interested in the tomatoes, "Try these; they are good." Now I wait and cook them when no one is around so I don't have to share. Even when my daughter comes from Texas, I waited for her to visit her girlfriend and made them while she was gone.

I love the Christmas season and miss all the traditions we did with our children over the years preparing for Christmas day. Most of the traditions were centered on the children, and now they have homes of their own and started traditions with their children. Even Santa changed his day of coming around to all the houses in our town from Christmas Eve to the 23rd. I decided it was time for Tom and me to start our own Christmas traditions. I talked Tom into being an ambassador of Christmas cheer and spread good will to everyone we came in contact with. The plan was to say "Merry Christmas" to whoever we made eye contact. The first person I approached was Scrooge and the second totally ignored me. But I plugged on. It was my mission I was the ambassador of Christmas, after all.

After forty-nine years, I finally met someone who felt the same disappointment at the Niagara Falls as I did. A while back, I was checking out at a restaurant and the cashier noticed the picture of the Niagara Falls on the front of my sweatshirt. She replied, "Niagara

Falls was really a disappointment to me. The way everyone builds it up so much I expected to see this gigantic waterfall and when I finally went to the falls they weren't anything like what they made them out to be." I said, "I feel exactly the same way. I heard so much about them and had high expectations. When I went they weren't what I envisioned either." I could have spent more time talking to her because our thinking was similar,—and believe me. I haven't found many people who think like me—but a line was forming behind me and I had to leave. Too bad. Finally, someone had some sense!

We recently celebrated our 50th class reunion. The festivities started on a Thursday when a celebrity from our class arrived from California to autograph his photographs at a local tavern. He acts in many of the shows we watch on television. It's always a pleasure to brag about graduating with him when he appears on a show. We stood in line to get his autograph with our classmates and fans that follow his career.

Friday night we met at a local club for cocktails, appetizers and small conversation. It was fun trying to identify our classmates as they walked through the door. Even after fifty years there was something you could recognize, such as the eyes, smile, or their personalities, especially after they talked a while. Watching classmates recognize each other throughout the evening was entertaining.

It seemed for some it was a time to get things off their minds that were festering for fifty years. A classmate approached a fellow and chewed him out for standing her up at the skating ring fifty-three years ago. He was speechless. She told him how difficult it was for her to get to the skating ring back in the day, just to be stood up. He apologized and stated he couldn't remember the incident. She continued, "I had a crush on you. What attracted me to you was you were a bad boy." He replied, "I wasn't a bad boy." Everyone around laughed and said, "Yes, you were." A bad boy back in those days said naughty words, acted tough, wore long hair, wore his pants below his waist, and smoked cigarettes.

Two classmates, the retired police chief from the next town and the president of our local bank, were standing by my table talking. I looked up and noticed they were dressed exactly alike, right down to their sandals. They had on pale yellow sport shirts, and red, green, blue, white, and yellow plaid shorts. I couldn't believe my eyes! I immediately got up and informed Tom. He went over to take a picture of them. By this time, everyone had noticed and there was quite a commotion. It was hilarious. At first they didn't know what all the fuss was about. Before long, someone informed them. They hadn't even noticed that they were dressed alike until someone pointed it out. They were good sports and just smiled and posed so everyone could take a memorable picture.

A few of us sat around a table until 1:30 in the morning talking about the good old days. The guys talked a lot about football. My favorite story was when they were at a game and the first player ran out of the building and fell and the rest of the team all fell in a pile. I could just picture this situation. In spite of this, we had a pretty good team. It's amazing how you can pick up where you left off with people you haven't seen for years; before long, we were all sixteen again.

Saturday night was a more formal occasion with dinner and dancing. The wives of the two characters who accidently dressed alike Friday night secretly got together and dressed them alike for the dinner dance. This time it was intentional. When they found out they just looked at their wives in disbelief. I just had to get their picture. This time they weren't too agreeable. Finally, they relented and unenthusiastically posed.

It was an enjoyable evening chatting with our classmates, especially the one I hadn't seen in fifty years. Before we ended the evening, we discussed having a party when we turn seventy.

The next morning over breakfast, Tom and I recaptured the enjoyable weekend and reminisced how far we have come since graduation. We marveled at how we managed to raise three remarkable children and they in turn are raising five amazing children in spite of our parenting, cartooning, and logic.

Our daughter, Maureen, met her husband, Mike, in college and they married four years after she graduated. They have three children and live in Denton, Texas. Maureen is a teacher and Mike is a sports editor at the Dallas Morning News. He is studying to be a paralegal, since the newspaper industry is taking a turn for the worst because of many turning to the Internet for news.

Lora, our daughter, brought a fellow, Jason, home she met in college. We didn't want to discourage him since he was the closest to a human that Lora brought home in a long time. Even when Jason backed into our car in the driveway, Tom said, "It is okay," especially because Tom and I had also done it. We understood perfectly how easy this could happen. We were very careful not to disclose any of Lora's bad habits or disagreeable behavior. We always praised her in his presence and pointed out her good points. Then before long our second daughter was married. She is a counselor and her husband is an X-ray technician. They have two children, Emory who she named after her Cabbage Patch doll, and Hattie, who was named after Jason's grandmother.

Our son, Marty, is now a major in the army and is involved in the space program. He has been stationed in Germany, Korea, Iraq, California, Seattle, New York, Virginia, and is currently stationed in Maryland. He is still single. He seems to be looking for that perfect girl. I told him she doesn't exist. I see the priesthood in his future.

Marty is still harassing his father. The last time he was home he put a red plastic ball in the tomato plants. Later, Tom looked into the backyard and said, "Look a tomato is ripe on that plant." Then he went out to get it. Watching him walk toward the plants and his expression when he picked up the red ball was priceless.

Some things never change. Tom still perceives the world differently than me, and we function like complete opposites. He is spontaneous and I research and plan my transactions well in advance. He is a spendthrift and I am frugal. He drinks beer for medicinal purposes and I drink prune juice. He enjoys reading his high-tech information on his computer in the noisy coffee shop, while I enjoy reading my book in the quiet, tranquil park. I love to go to the movie theater, and he would rather sit home and watch reruns on the television. However, there are a few things we agree upon. We want everything to be perfect now-a-days, not too hot or too cold. We both enjoy relaxing in our long-johns sipping on a warm cup of tea with lemon and munching on homemade cookies while watching reruns of our favorite shows on cold winter nights. Unfortunately, we usually fall asleep during the commercials. A few times a week we relax at our favorite coffee shop in the morning and our favorite tavern in the early evening.

Tom survived heart surgery, prostate cancer, and I survived a hip replacement. We were friends since we were twelve years old and we have managed to stay married forty-nine years by seeing the humor in everyday living. If these stories hint that we are *cartoon characters*, then so be it. Even though we are complete opposites, we are in complete harmony; we have something going here. We are two minds with one thought and keep on living the comic strips, Lally Logic, and Liz Logic that no one understands but us. Tom still hasn't figured out what makes me tick. TICK, TOCK, TICK TOCK!